The Pegasus Ledgers

A J Marlow

NCC Blackwell

MANCHESTER • OXFORD

British Library Cataloguing in Publication Data

Marlow, A. J.
(Andrew J.)
    The Pegasus Ledgers
    1. Computers systems software
    I. Title
    005.3
ISBN 0-85012-794-7

Published for NCC Publications by NCC Blackwell Ltd.

Editorial Office: The National Computing Centre Ltd, Oxford Road, Manchester M1 7ED, England.

NCC Blackwell Ltd, 108 Cowley Road, Oxford OX4 1JF, England.

Typeset in 11pt Dutch using Aldus PageMaker version 3.0 and a Hewlett Packard LaserJet series II; and printed by Hobbs the Printers of Southampton.

ISBN   0-85012-794-7

Acknowledgements

I would like to thank the many individuals at Pegasus Software Limited who have assisted in both the production of this book, and have provided essential technical information in the past which has gone towards the content indirectly. At Pegasus, thanks are due to Clive Booth (managing director) who has given his enthusiasm and support to the publication, Andrea Hart (publications manager) for permission to reproduce illustration material from the current Pegasus manuals, Steve Adkins (technical development assistant) a guru of accounting knowledge and in-depth function of the software, and Frank Bentley (training manager). I am also grateful to former Pegasus employees who provided much of the technical background on the software and to whom I make apologies for any misrepresentation of their otherwise accurate and clear information — Johnnie Johnson (former managing director) the designer of the original Pegasus business software suite, Marcus Pinny (former technical director), Jim Bird (former development manager), and Bob Page (former training manager).

I am also grateful to those at NCC Blackwell who are responsible for the production of the book, including Geoff Simons, Marcia Lamb, Clare Fisher and Nicola Eaton.

This, and all other books I have had the pleasure of writing, owe much to the dedication of Brenda Durndell, who provides invaluable assistance in the preparation of manuscripts and artwork.

Preface

There are over 40,000 registered Pegasus users throughout the country, with many more potential business users and training organisations that will be using Pegasus for their accounting and accounts training operations. For this large number of users, there has been little or no additional guidance and information about the product range, outside the standard documentation that accompanies the software. This book aims to go one step towards bridging the gap between the straightforward functional instructions that a user manual provides and the kind of in-depth discussion that takes place in a training environment, or as a result of a conversation with a technical support individual with extensive knowledge and experience of the accounting ledgers of Pegasus.

The ledger modules of sales, purchase and nominal have been chosen as the subject matter for this publication because, with the possible exception of payroll, they form the core of the accounting system about which the most questions are asked. They also represent the modules that sell in the largest numbers and therefore are likely to be of interest to the widest readership. The areas that give most difficulties to users − the analysis functions, integration and report generator − are discussed from a different angle from that used in the documentation and with a different style of presentation. It is the intention that by reading about these facilities, a user can begin to understand more about the software package than would otherwise be obtained by reading the documentation alone. For the newcomer, an introduction to the principal purposes of the ledgers and the main functions provided by the Pegasus software modules is given.

In addition, some technical information is provided about the files and data processing aspects of the software. How do transactions and master records link together? is just one of the questions answered, with Appendix B giving an example of how it is done. This information is not essential to the operation of the software, but often arises in technical support situations, and a user who is armed with such details is likely to be better equipped to understand the nature of problems and their solutions.

The book can be read by both users and potential users alike, but it is mainly intended to provide an enhancement to documentation and training received by existing users. To this end, the book assumes a certain knowledge of basic information already covered in the manuals, as well as expanding on this same information in the hope that a fuller understanding will result.

Throughout the book, reference is made to both the Single-User and Senior product ranges. Where specific differences occur, these are mentioned, but you should check that the facilities described are included in your software before trying out any suggestions. In Appendix A, a list of some of the more significant differences between the Senior and Single-User sales, purchase and nominal ledgers is given. It is also important to understand that the software is constantly being revised by Pegasus Software Limited, and it is possible, therefore, that features mentioned may change. Also, it is possible that a user reading this book may have a version of the software which is, by now, out of date, and will therefore not necessarily relate to every topic discussed. As far as possible, however, I have tried to cover areas in as general a way as possible, but neither Pegasus Software Limited, nor the publishers can accept responsibility for the accuracy of the content of this book in respect of previous, current or future versions of the software.

A Marlow, MSc
Titchmarsh, 1989

Contents

1 Introduction

The history of Pegasus Software Limited began in the late 1970s at the beginning of the microcomputer industry's own history. It began within an organisation then called Brikat Developments (Holdings) Limited, which owned a distributor of microcomputer hardware and software trading under the name of HB Computers. Shortly after HB Computers began trading, it became apparent to the directors that the success of any microcomputer sales operation was dependent to a large extent on the quality and availability of its software, and in mid-1979, Johnnie Johnson was recruited from the computer department of an international company to write bespoke software for HB Computers' customers. However, this was not a cost effective approach to supplying software, so Mr Johnson designed off-the-shelf software packages known as HB Ledgers, first launched by Brikat in 1979.

In late 1980, Commodore Business Machines (UK) Limited introduced a new range of microcomputers known as the CBM 8000 series. To take advantage of this development, the HB Ledgers were rewritten and launched under the name Pegasus. Sales of these packages were significantly better than anticipated and, in December 1981, Pegasus Software Limited was formed as a wholly owned subsidiary to control and develop this growing aspect of the group's business. It was headed by Johnnie Johnson, who took the role of the company's managing director.

During 1982 and 1983, the company carried out a detailed

investigation of the North American software market, and this led to the development of specifically tailored versions of the Pegasus accounting packages which were launched in 1983 under the name of Osprey through a 90% owned US subsidiary, Osprey Business Software Inc.

By 1984, interest was taken in the Pegasus products by IBM United Kingdom Product Sales Limited, and the software was adopted by IBM as one of its own PC software offerings for accounting, and this strengthened the already considerable sales of the software within the United Kingdom. Also in that year, the holding company, now called Brikat Group, was placed on the unlisted securities market.

Up to this time, the accounting modules of the Pegasus business suite of software were designed for use on single microcomputers, and as such appealed mainly to the smaller businesses in terms of both cost and functions. However, during the latter half of 1984, Pegasus Software Limited developed a new range of accounting modules which were designed for multi-user and networked computers, and took advantage of the new development period to enhance the features of the software considerably compared to the standard product offering. This new range was called Pegasus Multi-User and the standard single-user Pegasus product range adopted the name of Pegasus Single-User by default.

The Multi-User product range incorporated many accounting and business features that were likely to be required by the larger company, including foreign currency accounting, multiple location stock control and extensive facilities for invoicing, order processing and nominal accounting. The first ledger modules of this range were launched at a specially organised event in March of 1985. This new range of software was also to be adopted by IBM who marketed the product under its own brand name — Teamwork. This new range of products, whilst being designed to provide for a multi-computer environment, proved to be successful as a single-user product in its own right, surpassing the sales of the entry level single-user product range. This made the nomenclature somewhat difficult to handle, and a new marketing initiative was to see the Multi-User range of products re-branded under the name of Pegasus Senior, which survives today. The standard single-user product range continues to sell well, but the overall best selling range has remained the Senior accounting modules in both single- and multi-user forms.

The success of the product ensured that Pegasus Software Limited provided the most significant turnover for the Brikat Group, despite the Group's considerable investment and diversification into the setting up of a number of microcomputer retail outlets, technical services facilities, and office supplies and equipment distributorships. This investment was not to be fruitful however, and Pegasus Software Limited was to shoulder the losses of many subsidiary companies during these difficult times in the market. A significant restructuring of activities and a massive rationalisation programme saw the departure of most of the Group's directors, including Colin Stanley who founded the organisation in 1973. The number of subsidiary companies in the Group dropped from some 26 to only four main profit-making enterprises, headed by Pegasus Software Limited.

New leadership and financial interest came in the form of Advent Limited, venture capitalists who took some 25% of the shares in the company and provided a new group chairman and a non-executive director. Together with other new directors on the board, the Group turned in significant results at the end of the rationalisation period, which saw a turnover decreased by almost £3 million, but an increase in profits, largely due to the fact that the financial clout behind the success of Pegasus products no longer had to support a loss-making programme of diversification. To mark this turnabout in the Group's affairs, the organisation changed its name to Pegasus Group plc, which clearly focussed attention on the main activities on which the Group has built ever since — business software.

After further reshuffling of responsibilities, Derek Moon, the previous non-executive group chairman, took on the role of chief executive officer, and Johnnie Johnson was appointed as technical director on the Group's main board, which made way for a

new managing director of Pegasus Software Limited. The new
man was Clive Booth, who, from a background in a leading
microcomputer dealership, built on the strength of the Pegasus
market penetration, and took the company into even higher
profits using a clearly defined strategy which maximised the
effectiveness of the dealer channel through which the company's
products had always been sold.

Today, Pegasus Software Limited, with its range of business
accounting software products, remains one of the most significant
suppliers of microcomputer software. It had previously even man-
aged to outsell Lotus 1-2-3 in the United Kingdom according to
several surveys. While the market and the competition have
grown, Pegasus products have retained a reputation for being easy
to use; a 'feature' of the software package that is of great import-
ance to the novice user, and can be as important as any operating
features that may or may not otherwise be present. In this respect,
Pegasus has remained a favourite system for first-time installation
of business software for many dealers and customers alike.

In the following chapters of this book, some of the most flexible
features of the accounting ledgers are discussed; those that often
get only superficial attention when the software is first set up, but
which, with further investigation, can enhance the effectiveness of
the information stored in your computer. The analysis facility is a
good example of this.

Before each of the three core ledger modules is dealt with in
turn, the following chapter gives you an in-depth view of the way
in which the accounting system functions — information not provided within the documentation. Indeed, this information is not
necessary for the basic operation of your software but, by providing an understanding of the way in which the processing of your accounting information is achieved, helps you to get much more
from your system, and helps you solve problems and difficulties
that would otherwise remain mysterious. This is especially important when dealing with suppliers and technical support people who
(at least should) already have that knowledge, on which to base
their recommendations and advice for the successful operation of

the software. You will not only benefit from this additional information in enhancing the output from your system, but will be better informed if you need to call upon technical assistance in the formative period of installation and initial use.

A separate chapter is devoted to both the integration and analysis facilities of the Pegasus Single-User and Senior products; two areas which are likely to vary the most from one user to another, and consequently the most difficult to get to grips with. Part of the reason why these areas of operation prove to be difficult for users, when so much of the rest of the package is so easy to use, is the fact that these subjects are encountered during the setting up stage of the software and, once defined, are rarely altered. This means that just when you are beginning to understand the concepts of analysis and integration, the knowledge is quickly forgotten as it does not form part of your regular processing activities. For many users, the analysis and integration requirements of the software are handled by the dealer as part of the installation process. Thus, the user never gets the opportunity to experiment with the features, and may not get around to questioning whether the analysis of their sales and purchases, for example, offers the most informative data in respect of their business operations.

The report generator is another example of a powerful feature that can often be overlooked by the user who, while quite content with the reporting options offered in the standard menus of the accounting system, may not have realised the potential of more specific and focussed reporting based on the data already stored in the files.

All in all, this book is about making the Pegasus accounting software work even harder for you. In order for this to be achieved, additional information about the product, over and above that provided in the manuals, and some examples are required to whet your appetite and prompt ideas for getting effective management control of your business accounts. You must be prepared to experiment as well as read, however, and you will only realise the best from your system when you are prepared to put in some effort of your own. The sample data files supplied with your Pegasus accounting software may help you in this respect, but for the most part you are advised to set up some data files of your own, using a unique company identifier, for the purpose of testing out ideas. Further guidance is given about this later in the book.

If you wish to seek additional information about Pegasus products, your supplier may be able to offer additional training. Pegasus Software Limited themselves will also be able to advise you of approved training centres for users, and if you have many staff to train, this may well be worth further investigation.

A book such as this is intended to serve as backup information to both the training you may receive and the documentation that accompanies the software. In particular, users in organisations where several staff are involved in using the computerised accounting facilities may benefit from information being presented in this way, which can be digested informally. The book also ensures that background knowledge is preserved for future users, in the event of current operating staff leaving the company or moving on to other roles within the organisation.

As a final point in this introduction, it should be understood that both the Single-User and Senior product ranges are covered in the text. The differences in the operation of these products are explained where relevant, so that it is obvious which product range is being discussed. While it is likely that you are using only one of the two product ranges, it may be of benefit to appreciate the functional differences, particularly if you are using the Single-User product, as you may learn that the Senior range offers some useful additional features which may warrant further investigation and discussion with your supplier. For those using the Senior product range, it is intended that the coverage of Single-User provides a suitable introduction to the more complex and diverse features of the Senior products which, in most cases, are extensions of well tried and tested functions of the Single-User product range in the first place. You are advised, therefore, to read all the preliminary information about the general facilities within the software before reading selectively for either product range.

2 The Pegasus Systems

Pegasus provides your ledger 'books' in the form of computer software and the data stored in your files on the disk drives of your microcomputer. There are three Pegasus ledgers in all:

— sales ledger;

— purchase ledger;

— nominal ledger.

Each of these ledgers provides the facilities to store certain types of information which relate to the everyday business transactions that a company makes: invoices, receipts, payments, credit notes, refunds and sundry adjustments to the accounts.

These ledgers, and indeed all Pegasus business accounting software packages, are supplied in 'modules'. This means that, with a couple of exceptions, each package may be used on its own, ie without having to be linked to any other. So, for a company requiring just the facilities of sales and purchase ledgers, only these two modules need to be purchased. However, as a modular system which can be integrated, many users benefit more by 'linking' the modules together, so that information entered in one ledger can be passed to another, without the need to enter it again. The nominal ledger, for example, will accept information from both the sales and purchase ledgers, so that the accounts for sales

17

and expenditure can be automatically updated with the values of the invoices and credit notes raised for the customers and received from the suppliers respectively.

THE PROGRAMS

On the program disks supplied by Pegasus Software are the program files relating to the appropriate modules. The number of program files depends upon the module, but as a general rule each program relates to one option on the main menu of the module concerned. For example, the sales ledger program that controls the setting up of the parameters is separate from the one which prints reports.

The disk names for programs follow the form shown below:

<program name>.EXE

The program name will depend upon the module, and includes a number which identifies the option number on the module's main menu for which the program provides control. For sales ledger the program names are as follows:

Single-User	Senior
SL1-9.EXE	PGSL1.EXE
SL2-9.EXE	PGSL2.EXE
SL3-9.EXE	PGSL3.EXE
SL4-9.EXE	PGSL4.EXE
SL5-9.EXE	PGSLP.EXE
SL6-9.EXE	

The programs SL1-9 and PGSL1 relate to option number 1 on the sales ledger main menu, which in both Single-User and Senior is the processing option, which covers name and address update routines, postings and enquiries; hence the programs control the processing of new customer accounts, the maintenance of existing accounts, the posting of invoices, credit notes, receipts, etc and account enquiries.

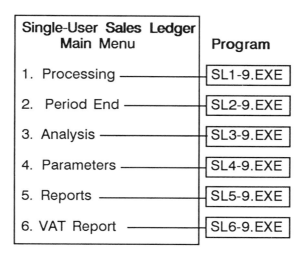

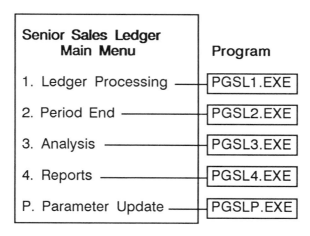

Figure 2.1 Programs and Menu Option Relationships

The programs SL2-9 and PGSL2 relate to option number 2 on the sales ledger main menu which, again for both product ranges, is the period-end routine. Other program names relate to menu options in a similar way, as shown in Figure 2.1. Note that Senior uses the option P for parameters, rather than option 4 which is used in Single-User.

Programs and their relationship to menu options for all other Pegasus modules work in the same way as illustrated for sales ledger. Only the main menus of the modules have associated programs, however. The sub-menu of the reports option, for example, carries several options for individual reports, but each of these is included in the one program for all reports. The file extensions of the program files are all .EXE. This indicates that the file is *executable*; in other words, a program that can be executed.

In addition to the program files that are concerned with the actual functions of the module menu options themselves, there are two other important programs, without which none of the other programs can be used:

Single-User   **Senior**   **Description**

PEGLO-9.EXE PGLOAD.EXE The 'loader' program
MENU-9.EXE   PGMENU.EXE The main menu program

The loader program is the one which is used to start up Pegasus from the operating system. It displays the Pegasus banner, version number, etc, and then automatically loads the menu program. The menu program presents the date and company identifier boxes as shown in Figure 2.2.

Figure 2.2   Date and Company Identifier Boxes

Once this screen of information is completed the main menu, which displays the program modules available to you, is presented. The menu program also performs all the utility functions, such as file lists, colour configuration, etc, and holds all the main menus of the modules themselves, and only when one of the options for a main menu is selected is a program for that module executed.

THE COMPANY IDENTIFIER

The company identifier is the mechanism that enables Pegasus to keep separate files of data for different companies or divisions, in the same disk partition or directory. It achieves this by placing a single character in front of all the data file names, according to the character that you enter in the company identifier box. So, when you accept the default of A, all data files subsequently created by the parameter routine (when the system is first used for that identifier) have the letter A at the beginning of the file name. For example:

ASL-NAME.DAT

Should the company identifier be changed, then a new set of data files needs to be created. This means setting up the parameters for a new 'company' and generating files with a different letter at the front. If that letter was B, for example, then the resulting file names would be preceded by the letter B, thus:

BSL-NAME.DAT

This ensures that the data stored in each file is maintained quite independently, and allows up to 26 different sets of data (one for each letter of the alphabet) to be stored in the same disk directory or partition. It is important to qualify the fact that they can be stored in the same directory, since Pegasus programs do not generally detect data files that are stored in a different directory from the programs (Unix and Xenix systems excepted). However, if the microcomputer being used has different partitions (also known as *virtual volumes*) which act like different disk drive letters (A, B, C, D, etc), then it is possible to store separate data files for different companies in various drive partitions. Pegasus programs automatically search all possible drive letters (but not sub-directories) for data, and this enables sets of data files with the same company identifier to be kept independently in different partitions, though this is not advisable, as it can easily lead to confusion. However, it is quite feasible to store different sets of data files with the same company identifier on separate floppy disks, provided they can be accommodated on the disk space available.

Data files are created, ready for use, when the parameters of a module are completed for the first time. Since the parameters can include files that contain the designs of document layouts, such as statements, remittance advices (both Senior only), invoices, payslips, etc, which may also be applicable to another company's data files, it may be useful to copy the relevant parameter files of one company to another identifier before adding names, addresses and transactions. For example, if using Pegasus on a DOS-based microcomputer, this can be done by setting up the parameters of the first company (A, for example), including all the relevant design layouts, and copying the files using the following operating system command:

    copy a*.dat b*.dat

This duplicates all the data files (which have the file extension .DAT) and at the same time replaces the first character of the duplicated files with the letter B.

It is important to note that this is best carried out prior to adding any master records (such as names and addresses) or transactions. Once transactions are recorded, they cannot be removed separately from the account records (both can be removed however, leaving only the parameters) without individually adjusting the balances and allocating the transactions, then carrying out a period-end routine.

THE DATA FILES

The data files are those in which the information about a

company's accounts are stored, rather like the files in a filing cabinet. Each module of Pegasus keeps its own set of data files, and if different company identifiers are being used, the additional data files are stored for each company.

The file names used for storing data are not actually seen by a user when using the Pegasus programs. The data file maps, provided as a utility function of the programs, only display the names of the modules to which data files belong. The actual data file names are made up as follows:

<company id><module code><file name><file extension>

For example, the following is the name of a sales ledger data file, which stores the names and addresses of the customers, ie the account details entered through the account name and address update routine:

Single-User   **Senior**

ASL-NAME.DAT   ASLPNAME.DAT

The only difference here between the file names of Single-User and Senior data files is the letter P in place of the hyphen, and this is really only a technical addition on the part of Pegasus Software Limited, so that they can identify the difference between files of the two product ranges.

The first character, then, is the company identifier ('A' in the above examples). This is followed by a module code. Each module of the Pegasus accounting system is identified by a two-character mnemonic, and they are:

SL	sales ledger	WG	payroll (wages)
PL	purchase ledger	FA	fixed assets
NL	nominal ledger	PS	retail (POS)
IN	invoicing	RP	report generator
ST	stock control	SH	sales history
AS	BOM (assemblies)	JC	job costing

This module code is then followed by either a hyphen (in the case of Single-User products) or a letter P (for Senior products).

The next part of the data file name is the word or mnemonic which identifies the nature of the contents of the file. In the previous example, the word NAME indicates that the data file contains the information maintained by the account name and address update routine. The same is used for sales, purchase, nominal and stock control modules, although in the case of nominal ledger, for example, the account update routine is actually referred to as an account 'header' update (since nominal accounts do not strictly have 'names' and certainly not addresses).

The following is a list of some of the file names that one might encounter among the data file names. All are four characters long:

Name	Description
NAME	account name (header) file, or stock item file
INDX	index file (described later)
FREE	file used for networking (described later)
PARM	parameter file
TRAN	transaction file
ANAL	analysis file
LETT	debtors letter content file
NLRP	nominal ledger profit and loss/balance sheet report designs
STAT	statement design file
REMT	remittance advice file
etc	

The file extension of all data files in Pegasus products is .DAT (short for data), with the only exception being the control and design files of report generator, which are described further in Chapter 7. The following paragraphs describe how these data files are used and briefly how the information is maintained within them. It is intended to help you understand a little about how Pegasus operates without being too technical, and such information may be useful in case of difficulties that require support from your supplier or from Pegasus Software Limited themselves.

HOW THE DATA FILES WORK

The data files store the information that you enter, new information which is calculated by the programs based on the information you enter, and special data which is used only by the programs in the organisation of the files and their contents.

The Parameter File

This is the file that contains the details entered when you set up the parameters of any Pegasus module. As you may be aware, the parameters are the first stage in setting up the data files of any of the Pegasus accounting modules, and they contain your responses to questions about how the program will perform certain functions (the 'options') and certain static information, such as your company name and address (used for report headings, for example), the type of printer that you use, the design of special documents (such as statements, remittance advices, etc) and in the case of Senior sales and purchase ledgers, descriptions for receipt/payment and adjustment types.

The parameter file itself is a *sequential* file. This means that the information stored within it is placed in sequence, and has no special indexing to locate information within it. The length (size) of the file is fixed according to the programs, so for each field you enter in the parameters of the module, there is a corresponding entry in the parameter file (even if this is a blank entry).

Apart from the actual information that you enter when you define a module's parameters, the parameter file also contains information placed there by the program. For example, the date the module's data files were last used is one of the first records in the parameter file. When you choose to carry out processing in, say, the sales ledger, the program will check the date the files were last used, and compare this with the computer's current system date. If it transpires that the system date is older than the date the files were last updated, the program displays a warning informing you of a date inconsistency, just in case you are inadvertently processing with the wrong system date. So, this parameter entry, though never actually seen by the operator, and not displayed on the screen when you set up your parameters, does exist in the parameter files and is used by the programs. Similarly, there are other parameter entries that are used for technical reasons, and which are not displayed in the parameters. One of these is the 'generation' number — a particularly important parameter entry when it comes to integrating the sales and purchase ledgers. It has been known to cause difficulties for some users of Pegasus programs, and is therefore explained in detail in Chapter 6 on integration.

Because the parameter file is essential to the successful operation of the module, no processing whatsoever is permitted within any of the modules until the parameters are set up. When an option is chosen from the main menu of a module, the programs check to see if the parameter file for the selected module resides on the disk. For example, if you choose to select a sales ledger processing option from the main menu of sales ledger, the program will search for the existence of ASL-PARM.DAT (assuming the company identifier used is A).

If this file cannot be found, the program assumes that you have the data files concerned on a floppy disk, and prompts you to insert a disk containing the sales ledger data files. The only time this does not happen, is when the parameter function is selected from the main menu. In this case, if the parameter file does not already exist, then the programs assume that a new set of data files are to be created for the selected module, and the operator is asked if this is a new file before proceeding any further.

So, the existence of a parameter is the factor which determines whether any further processing can take place, and when an operator has finished entering all of a module's parameter details for the first time, the programs automatically create all the other data files required for processing. These are created as 'empty' files, ready for the next stage in the processing of a module's data, including the name file, transaction file, index file, etc.

The Names File

In most cases, the next stage for an operator, having set up the module parameters, is to enter details about customers, suppliers, nominal accounts, etc. These are clearly needed before any transactions can be entered on the system, as the names file contains the details of the accounts (in the case of sales, purchase and nominal ledgers). For each account, whether a customer, supplier or nominal account, a single account record is stored in the NAME file.

Each record has a corresponding record number. As accounts are added to the file, a new record is created and added on to the end of the file (see Figure 2.3).

Names File

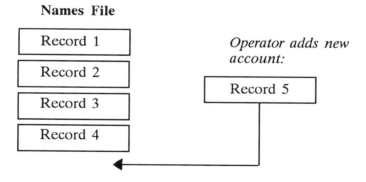

Figure 2.3   Adding New Names Records

If an existing account record is recalled for amendment, then, once amended, it is replaced in the same record location within the data file. Only new records are added to the end. This means, however, that the order in which accounts are listed, when they are printed from the names file, is that in which they are entered, rather than any other order, such as account name or number. This situation is rectified when a month- or period-end procedure is carried out, when all records are sorted into account number order, so that their corresponding record numbers in the names file may change as a result. Closely associated with the names file is the index file.

The Index File

This file provides the mechanism which enables programs to locate names records within the system in a fast and efficient manner. Unlike purely sequential files, which have to be read sequentially (ie record by record) until the desired record is located, the index file provides a faster way of locating an account. The index file contains all of the account numbers of the ledger names records and a corresponding record number which identifies to the program where the appropriate name record can be found in the names file.

Searching through a file which contains only account numbers and a record number is a much faster way of locating an account than reading through all the account details. When the operator enters an account number in order to call up, say, a sales ledger account, the program looks in the index to see if the account number entered actually exists. If it does not exist in the index file, the program immediately returns an error message on the screen to indicate that the account record does not exist. If the account number is found, then the index will provide the program with the record number corresponding to the names file where the remaining account details will be found. This is known as 'addressing'. The index file gives the *address* of the account in the names file, so that the program can go straight to that account without having to read through any other, irrelevant, records.

Like the names file, the index has to be reorganised when the period-end procedure is carried out, since the record numbers of the accounts will have changed. When a corruption occurs on data involving the names and addresses files, for example in the case of a power or computer failure, it is usually the case that the record number associated with an account number in an index does not give the address to a corresponding account record in the names file. In other words, the index has become corrupted, and can no longer provide correct information about an account record's location. When the program subsequently tries to find the account in the names file, for which an invalid record number has been given by the index, the program knows that the data files are not properly organised, and responds by displaying a message to the effect that the files are corrupt, the next time an operator attempts to access that particular account.

While it is possible for trained technical support people and programmers to *mend* such a problem (by altering the data files and their record numbers), for most operators, the only course of action under such circumstances is to revert to a backup copy of their data files, taken prior to the occurrence that caused the corruption.

Pegasus programs provide special utility programs that enable you to check the validity or integrity of your data files, so that any corruptions can be spotted early. In the above example, a single corrupt record may not be noticed straight away, particularly if the account is not accessed for some time, and it may be that the problem is only discovered at the month-end, when the programs come to reorganise the data files. Hence, the file checks help the user to look for potential problems on a more regular basis, and the program which carries out the checks is simply making sure that all the cross referencing between records is valid.

There are similar links between account name records and their transactions, which also need to be maintained accurately, so that all the transactions for an associated account can be found easily, and this is described next.

The Transaction Files

The names file records, apart from holding all the details of an account as entered by the operator (such as name and address, credit limit, account type, etc), have a special field called a *pointer*.

A pointer is simply another type of 'address' which informs the program about where associated records can be found. The transaction file contains all the transaction records associated with the ledger concerned. In order that the programs know which transactions belong to particular accounts, special reference fields are used which give the address of the first, next, previous and last transactions for any given account record, and it is these references that are the *transaction pointers* (see Figure 2.4).

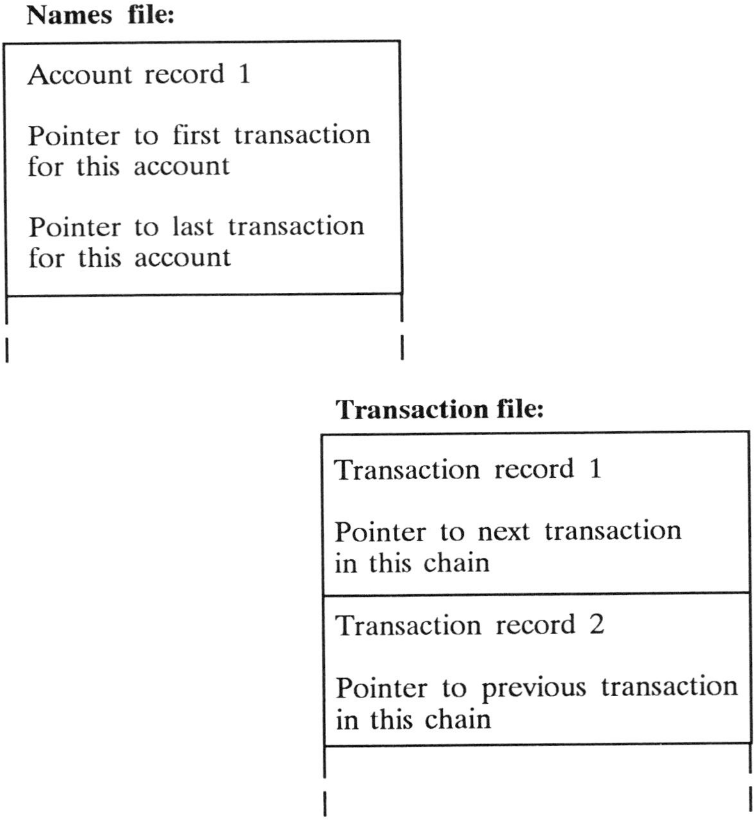

Names file:

Account record 1

Pointer to first transaction
for this account

Pointer to last transaction
for this account

Transaction file:

Transaction record 1

Pointer to next transaction
in this chain

Transaction record 2

Pointer to previous transaction
in this chain

Figure 2.4   Transaction Pointers

The pointers ensure that when an account enquiry is displayed, for example, the pointer in the account record within the names file indicates to the program where to find the first transaction belonging to that account in the transaction file. That transaction will indicate the address (location) of the next transaction for the account, and so on. Thus, a chain of transactions are pieced together which all belong to the same account. When the last transaction for the account is reached, no further transactions are searched for. Hence, the simple act of displaying the transactions belonging to an account on an enquiry screen, activates a whole series of record locating through the transaction file.

The actual transaction records themselves hold details that identify the type and value of a transaction. The 'transaction type' is actually a code field stored along with a transaction which identifies to the program whether the transaction is an invoice, credit note, receipt, payment, adjustment or whatever. This code is not actually seen by the operator when a transaction is being processed, but is stored as part of the transaction record, as are the pointer fields. The code usually takes the form of a single letter or number. For example, here are some transaction types typically stored in a ledger transaction file:

— I   invoice;

— C   credit note;

— D   discount;

— B   balance;

— R   receipt;

— U   unallocated receipt.

In addition to the codes, the transaction record holds the value of the transaction, as either a positive or a negative figure, depending upon whether the entry was a debit or a credit. The operator does not actually enter the sign of a value when processing a transaction, but the program adds the + or − according to the type of transaction being processed. The date of a transaction is stored, and so is the number of the day in the month (for example, 10th, 21st, 25th, etc) on which it is entered. This enables a list of transactions to be printed that were entered on a particular day in the month. If the operator chooses to print a list of 'Today's Invoices', this day number is referred to by the programs to ascertain whether a transaction should be included in the report or not, depending upon the system date prevailing at the time the report option was selected.

Transaction files are quite complicated, mainly due to the nature of the pointers which link all the transaction records together and relate them to particular account records. As with names files, power and computer failures are likely to result in file corruption, particularly when the failure occurs while a transaction processing function is being carried out. The reason the files become corrupt is simply because the pointers do not get linked up properly if a processing routine fails to be properly completed. If the transaction record points to a location in the file where there is no corresponding transaction record, the program responds with an error message informing the operator that the files are corrupt.

The fact that the transaction file has links with the names file is the reason why one cannot simply delete the transaction file on its own, and expect the account records to remain unaffected. For example, when using the Pegasus programs for the first time, many users experiment with test data before actually entering 'live' transaction information. However, it is common to enter actual customer, supplier or nominal account details (probably because they are not easy to invent for testing purposes). The result is that, after a short period of testing, when the user is ready to enter real data, the test transactions have to be removed first. Any attempt to delete the transaction file from the disk to achieve this will quickly result in the corruption of the files, preventing access to any of the accounts at all. The answer, therefore, is to set up the names and addresses of accounts first, then copy the data files at this stage, before adding any test transactions. Once testing and training has been completed, *all* files can be deleted and replaced with the backup copies which include the names and addresses, but no transactions. Live data can then be entered quite safely. Transactions can be removed individually by allocating and performing a period-end procedure, but this is a tedious method.

Transaction files are not sorted into order like names files at the month-end. They are maintained by the program according to the processing carried out, and new transactions are added to the end of the file, in the order in which they are entered. The parameter file of the module does store the number of the next available transaction location, which helps speed up the allocation of new transaction records.

At the month-end procedure, in the case of open item accounts, transactions are only removed from the sales and purchase ledgers if they are allocated. Transactions that are allocated have a different transaction type code to those that are not, hence the program can identify which transaction records to remove. In the case of balance forward accounts, transactions are removed that are not related to the new period for accounting, but a total balance is carried forward which relates to the aggregate value of transactions for each account concerned.

The Analysis File

Analysis files are those files of the sales and purchase ledgers that store the values of invoices and credit notes. These are used for both sales and purchase analysis reports and for transferring corresponding values to the accounts of the nominal ledger.

Unlike the transaction file, the analysis file does not have pointers to link analysis records to the other files in the module. The analysis file itself is only created when an invoice or credit note transaction is first posted to either of the ledgers. The information stored within the analysis file is based upon the analysis of an invoice or credit note in the ledger processing section. This means that there is one analysis record for every line of analysis which breaks down the total value of an invoice to a corresponding analysis code. The analysis code itself, which is described in more detail in Chapter 6, is actually made up of a combination of analysis codes, which together describe a value in some predefined way, and/or indicate its destination nominal account when it is transferred. The contents of the analysis file can be printed by choosing any of the user-definable analysis report options within the analysis sub-menu, then choosing the option to list all input, offered on all reports. The resulting printout includes every item in the analysis file, regardless of the selection criteria which apply to the chosen analysis report type.

The analysis file also contains a 'flag' or indicator which identifies the last record which was transferred to the nominal ledger. This ensures that, no matter how many times the analysis of sales and purchase ledgers to nominal ledger is carried out, only those transactions not previously transferred will be processed.

The month-end procedure actually deletes the analysis file, so all analysis reports and transfers to the nominal ledger have to be carried out prior to the month-end. A new analysis file is then created when the first invoice or credit note transaction is posted at the start of the new month.

Document Design Files

These types of data files are straightforward sequential files, like the parameter file. They contain a record for each line of a document's layout (for example, a statement format line) and are referred to whenever a document is to be printed. This means that the layout can be changed at any time, and the program will acknowledge the new layout the very next time an associated document is to be printed.

These files, which include the layout of the nominal ledger profit and loss and balance sheet reports, debtors letters, statements, remittance advices and cheque layouts, are not connected to any other files. Although they may be presented to the operator as part of the parameter functions of a module, the file created and maintained is quite independent of the main parameter file, and no harm is done in the event of such files being lost or inadvertently deleted (except that the design will need to be respecified). This means that the design files can be copied and used for different company identifiers, saving the rekeying of, say, a statement design for more than one set of data files. Once copied to another identifier, they can then be modified if required; the program treating them as if they were created for the data set concerned.

Search Index Files

These types of files are optionally created for Single-User modules, or automatically maintained for Senior modules. They are another index to the account records which are based not only on the account number, but a shorthand version of the account name. Up to 15 characters of the account names are used as a quick reference to the more comprehensive name of an account, and the search index in which these entries are stored, allows accounts to be accessed by entering all, or part of, this short name.

Like the normal index file, the search index stores the location of the account record so it can be found in the names file. The difference is that the input of a *search string* — some characters that can be located in the short name — is used to locate the index entry first. It also permits the 'scrolling' of accounts by flipping through the index file as if it were a card index system.

DATA FILES AND SIZES

The size of data files depends upon the number of records stored within them. This may sound like an obvious statement, but not all accounting packages maintain files in this way. In some cases, the size of a data file may have to be predetermined according to the maximum number of records you are expecting to need. In these cases, the data files will always occupy the maximum amount of disk space, regardless of whether the file is only half full of data.

With all Pegasus modules, both Single-User and Senior, the data files expand as new records are entered. This means that the amount of disk space that they occupy is dependent only upon the number of records stored. The sizes of the parameter and document files are fixed. The one point worth remembering about data files is that the month-end procedure duplicates the files while the reorganisation is carried out. The program creates a series of temporary files in which the reorganised data is stored. Once the month-end procedure has been completed, the operator is given the option of 'erasing the old files'. If the response to the prompt to continue with the month-end is affirmative, then the original files are deleted and the temporary files are renamed to become the files for the new month's processing. The consequence of this is that there must be sufficient disk space available to create the temporary files, and this means that whatever space is already occupied by the current data files will need to be free for the reorganisation procedure to take place.

NETWORKING AND MULTI-USER USE

Pegasus Single-User can be used on a network. This means that several microcomputers can be linked together, with one machine acting as a main source of programs and data (called the 'server' because it serves all the other computers). Pegasus programs include a special facility which prevents two or more users trying to update the same file of information at the same time when the programs are operated in a network environment. This is achieved by using what is called a FREE file. This is an 'empty' data file and there is one for each module. For example, the corresponding file for the sales ledger is ASL-FREE.DAT or ASLPFREE.DAT. This file contains no information as such, but is used as an indicator to the programs to find out whether any user is accessing the data files of a particular module. If, for example, one operator decides to post invoices to a sales ledger account, the program will look for the file ASL-FREE.DAT and rename it to ASL-LOCK.DAT. This status of the file indicates that the sales ledger data files are in use, and will remain the case until the operator concerned terminates the processing function and exits from the routine within the sales ledger. Once the operator exits the routine, the program will rename the file to ASL-FREE.DAT again, thus indicating that the sales ledger files are now free for use by other operators.

Should another user on the network decide to access the sales ledger data files while the files are already in use, the programs will not be able to detect the presence of the ASL-FREE.DAT file, since it will have been renamed to ASL-LOCK.DAT. This causes the program to display an error message to the second operator to inform them that access to the sales ledger files is denied. The second operator will then have to wait until such time as the files have become available for use (ie the FREE file returns) before being allowed access to the data file.

Not all access is denied, however, and other operators can carry out enquiries on accounts and print reports while other users are using the same module's data files. It is only during the act of updating the files, either by amending or adding account records, processing transactions or updating the parameters, that access is restricted to only one user at a time.

This free and lock file usage occasionally rears its head for users who are not networking their computers. Even when Pegasus Single-User is being used on a single microcomputer, the renaming of these files takes place anyway. The only occasion when a user might encounter a message which denies access to the data files because of the free file not being available, is in the event of a power or computer failure. Imagine the situation whereby a user is adding transactions to the sales ledger accounts through the ledger postings option, and a power failure interrupts the processing, or perhaps another person comes along and accidentally unplugs the computer. The FREE file will have been renamed to LOCK when the processing began, but because the operator did not have the chance to exit the routine satisfactorily, the file did not get renamed back to FREE. The consequence is that the next time the operator attempts to access the data files, this is denied, because the program cannot find the FREE file, and therefore believes that there is still another operator using the system, even though there is only one operator and one computer.

For true multi-user operation of an accounting system, this file locking process is inadequate. Larger companies that process many transactions per day, may require different operators to have access to the sales ledger data files at the same time. For example, an invoicing department may need to post invoices, while another handles the posting of receipts, and yet another updates account records. Clearly, the file locking procedure is not sufficient, since it enables only one operator to update files at any one time. Pegasus Senior, therefore, provides an additional level of restriction. The file locking is still used, especially in the case of an operator changing the parameter files. After all, the parameters control options and functions that can affect the entire ledger, so anyone making changes to the parameters will lock out all other users of the same module.

However, there is an additional locking procedure which is at record level. This means that an individual sales or purchase ledger account is locked while it is being used for processing, which prevents other users from updating the same account. However, like the file locking, it does not prevent the programs from reading information relating to the account, should another user wish to display an account enquiry or print a report while an account is being updated. Most importantly, several operators can all be using the ledger processing function and updating the same set of data files, but no two or more operators can update the same account record at the same time. Attempts to do so result in the display of an error message 'Account Active', and the operator must wait until the account is clear for use.

If such record locking were not used, the data files could easily be corrupted. Again, if Pegasus Senior is used on a single micro-computer, the locking facilities are still operating, and any encounter of error messages in association with active accounts or locked files is usually an indication of a system that has been closed down without the proper procedures of exit through the menu system.

The record locking of Pegasus Senior data files is achieved through the use of a single character in the account record and index files, which takes the form of a Y or N to indicate whether the account is active or not. Whenever access is requested for a particular account, the programs check the status of this indicator, and if the operator requesting access is doing so through a routine which is used to update the files, and the indicator is set to Y, the account will not be available for processing. Once processing of an account is completed, this indicator is reset to N by the programs, so that other operators may have access to it as required. No enquiry or reporting process checks the status of this indicator, since it does not matter whether an account is being processed while an account is being updated. However, the report or enquiry will not show any transaction record being processed at the time the account is accessed. Transactions are only added to the file when the operator exits from the processing routine, and returns to the menu.

3 The Nominal Ledger

Traditionally, book-keeping was based on three kinds of accounts: personal accounts, real accounts and nominal accounts. The personal accounts related to the accounts of the persons (or firms, or companies) with whom one traded. In a computerised system, such accounts are kept in the sales and purchase ledgers. The real accounts related to the assets of the company — 'real' things that could be considered tangible, whether it was a chair one sits on, or the building in which the business operated. Nominal accounts related to profit and loss items such as light and heat, wages and rents received, but because the word 'nominal' literally means 'in name only', the traditional view was that these nominal accounts contained values that were not actually there: while the wages account may show a value of £15,000, the staff may have already taken the wages home, and the account simply records the expense to the organisation.

Modern computer-based nominal ledgers, however, tend to cover some or all of the above account types. Strictly speaking, the nominal ledger is the 'general' ledger, and is used to record the totals of the personal accounts, the asset values and the profits and losses.

Computer-based nominal ledgers force a double-entry form of book-keeping. That is to say, the operator will not be permitted to post a journal without first ensuring that the total of debit values matches the total of credit values within the journal transaction.

41

With manual book-keeping systems, one has to rely on strict rules about the way in which entries are recorded in order to minimise the risk of posting an unbalanced entry. The trial balance plays an important role in ensuring that the total of all debit values within the accounts exactly matches the total of all the credit values.

For a computerised nominal ledger, the trial balance is largely irrelevant in this respect, since the totals will always balance by virtue of the fact that a transaction cannot be stored until the totals balance. The trial balance instead becomes an audit trail in its own right, providing a means of listing the balances of all accounts held in the nominal ledger, optionally with individual transaction details. As an extension to the trial balance, budget figures that are allocated to various accounts can be printed so that a comparison may be made between the actual account balance and the period budget at a given period-end.

NOMINAL POSTINGS

The nominal ledger records the following types of transaction:

— sales ledger postings;

— purchase ledger postings;

— journal entries.

They are all journals, in fact, but the sales and purchase values may be automatically transferred from the respective ledgers directly into specified nominal accounts (see also Chapter 6 on integration). Journal entries are a means of posting transaction values to any nominal account, or, more precisely, between nominal accounts. Once all the accounts themselves are set up, the journal entry facility (the processing section of the nominal ledger) can be used to record income and expenditure — profit and loss transactions — which enable you to arrive at a set of final accounts that show the status of your company's financial base.

The types of journal posted will range from petty cash, bank account entries, expense analysis, etc, through to asset values, liabilities and other balance sheet postings. There are special journal entries too, which are for the temporary postings needed for period accounting adjustments and prepayments and accruals.

DOUBLE-ENTRY METHOD

The double-entry posting method applies to computerised nominal ledgers in the same way as a manually maintained set of books. The general rule is:

— *debit the account that receives a value;*

— *credit the account that gives a value.*

Another way of putting the rule is 'debit the receiver and credit the giver'. By following this rule strictly, one can ensure that the balances of accounts are correctly maintained. One of the reasons people get into difficulty over this rule, particularly if they are not used to book-keeping, is the fact that they confuse debits and credits with their own personal bank statements. If you look at a bank statement, you will notice that the money that goes out of your account appears in the debit column, and the money that goes in appears in the credit column.

If you apply that to the case of a nominal ledger bank account, your debits and credits will actually be the wrong way round. In the nominal bank account, a debit balance indicates that the account is healthy, whereas a credit balance would indicate that you are overdrawn. This is because a receipt from, say, a customer, paid into your bank account would follows these rules:

— credit the customer account (which 'gives' the money);

— debit the bank account (which receives the money).

The principles of book-keeping become further complicated by the fact that there are sometimes many accounts involved in a sales transaction, including the customer account in the sales ledger, the nominal ledger sales account and the sales control account, also in the nominal ledger. All of these three are involved in the recording of an invoice within the Pegasus ledgers, which is difficult to reconcile when you consider that you must post only double-entries, yet you have only three accounts!

Part of the 'mystery' is due to the way in which a computer ledger system handles the transfer of transaction information between modules, while maintaining a balanced trial balance in the nominal ledger.

The nominal ledger which produces the trial balance *must* have two entries — a debit and a credit — for every transaction. In the case of a sales invoice posted in the sales ledger, one side of the double-entry is in the nominal account for sales, according to the way in which you analyse sales in the nominal (ie by product type, sales areas, or just into one consolidated sales account). This is the income account for the profit and loss statement. The other side of the double-entry is in the sales ledger control account and is actually the balance sheet item which represents the debtors amount (the current asset) showing how much is owed to you on paper.

When a receipt is posted, the amount received is posted, again, in two accounts within the nominal ledger. One side of the double-entry will be the bank account, the other side of the double-entry will be the sales control account. This time, the sales control account is reduced by the amount posted because you are reducing the amount owed by your customers (ie reducing the value of debtors).

The following example shows a sales invoice and receipt transaction and the corresponding debit and credit entries within the nominal ledger:

Invoice is raised for £1,000:

Credit the sales account   £1,000
Debit the sales control account   £1,000

Payment is received in full:

Debit the bank account	£1,000
Credit the sales control account	£1,000

The balance of the sales control account is now zero — ie no money is outstanding.

From this example, it can be seen that the value of the sales ledger control account (also referred to as the debtors control account) represents, at any given time, the actual amount of money owed by customers.

A similar situation applies in the case of suppliers and purchase accounts. A creditors (purchase) control account is held within the nominal ledger, and a corresponding purchase account holds the double-entry when a supplier's invoice is processed, thus:

Invoice received for £500:

Debit the purchase account	£500
Credit the purchase control account	£500

Payment is made in full:

Credit the bank account	£500
Debit the purchase control account	£500

The balance of the purchase control account is now zero — ie no money is owed to suppliers. From this example, it can be seen that the purchase control account (also referred to as the creditors control account) reflects the amount of money owed to suppliers at any one time. The purchase account is the profit and loss account used to indicate the expenditure made on goods or services received, whereas the control account is the balance sheet account which reflects the liability of the amount owed to suppliers.

By keeping strictly to the double-entry rule, you can see how the posting of corresponding entries affects the profit and loss situation of the accounts. It is equally clear that although the nominal ledger will ensure that a double-entry is made, it cannot prevent you from posting the debits and credits the wrong way round. Should this occur, you run the risk of misrepresenting the profitability and balance sheet status of your business's accounts. The best safeguard against this is simply to learn the rules, and pay attention to trial balance printouts which can show anomalies. For example, expense accounts almost invariably have debit balances. Should you spot a credit balance amongst a number of expense accounts, chances are that it has been incorrectly posted, and there will be another account with an incorrect posting of the corresponding amount.

JOURNALS

Journal entry routines provide a comment field which can be attached to each line (transaction) in a journal, as shown in Figure 3.1 below.

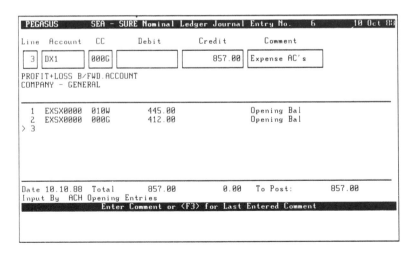

Figure 3.1   Journal Entry Screen

It is good practice to use this comment field to make clear not only the nature of the posting, but some indication of the corresponding account to which the double-entry will be made. This will make it easier to trace a misposting from one account to another.

The nominal ledger provides for the posting of special journal entries. These are entries which are generally used for temporary adjustments to the balances of certain accounts within the nominal ledger, prior to the production of a period profit and loss report.

Typical special journals are prepayments and accruals. For example, suppose you have paid rates for the next six months in advance, you have, in other words, made a prepayment. If the actual prepayment was made in June, and you produced a profit and loss report for either the period ending June or for the month of June alone, without any adjustments to the accounts, then your profit and loss report would not show a true figure. This is because you have reduced your profit in June by the amount of rates due between June and November. Strictly speaking, only one sixth of the total rates amount applies to June's accounts. Similarly, you would affect the profit in the following month by increasing the profit figure, when in fact another one sixth of the rates was due.

Adjusting for such circumstances is the purpose of the special journal entry. It enables the value of the account to be changed for the purpose of the current period, so that an accurate profit and loss statement can be produced. Once the period-end procedure has been run, this journal is automatically 'reversed'. The word reversed is in quotes since a reversing journal is not actually posted in the case of Pegasus Single-User, but the special journal is actually removed as if it were not made in the first place — ie the transaction does not remain stored on the accounts at all.

The important aspect, whether the journal is reversed or removed, is that it is a temporary journal which relates only to the current period. It cannot be a permanent posting, since the fact that the prepayment was made on a particular day cannot be altered. Only the temporary adjustment for reporting purposes is made and the transaction files, and consequently the trial balance are not affected by the posting. The following example shows what happens:

Rates account:

		Dr	Cr
1st June	Prepayment 6 mths	600	

For June's final accounts, the following special journal entry is recorded:

30th June	Rates account		500
30th June	Prepayment control	500	

Rates attributed to period ended 30th June are shown by the new 'temporary' status of the rates account:

		Dr	Cr
1st June	Prepayment 6 mths	600	
30th June	From special journal		500
30th June	Rates for this period	100	

It is the £100 that is used in the calculation of the profit/loss for the current period or period-to-date.

ACCOUNT CODES AND SET UP

By being integrated to the sales and purchase ledgers, the nominal ledger provides the core of the accounting processing of the entire business system. However, the integration of the sales and purchase ledgers does pose a question for most users when they first begin setting up the accounts. Which should be set up first, the nominal ledger or the sales and purchase ledgers?

The reason for this problem is the fact that the codes used in the nominal ledger can affect the choice of sales and purchase analysis codes, and vice versa. It is not realistic to insist that there is a right or wrong way, but for want of any better advice, the nominal ledger should take priority. A well structured set of nominal accounts is essential for clear management reporting, and, if properly arranged, can provide almost as much information as a sales or purchase analysis alone. This does not mean that the analysis codes should be ignored, and Chapter 6 deals with the integration and coding structures in more detail.

The nominal accounts themselves are arranged by account number. In the case of the Senior nominal ledger, accounts can be associated with cost centre codes too, which assist in the management of budget control by cost centre, and for profit and loss reporting. How the accounts are arranged is an important matter and deserves some forward planning. It is unlikely, however, that the chart of accounts that are defined when the nominal ledger is first set up will remain valid for long unless you are following a tried and tested coding system. The reason the allocation of account numbers is so important, is because it can provide a great deal of reporting flexibility if properly employed, especially when used in conjunction with the report generator, which allows selection criteria to be user-defined.

COST AND BUDGET CENTRES

A cost or 'profit' centre can be defined as a section of the organisation for the purposes of budgetary control. Strictly speaking, there is no such thing as a profit centre — only cost centres. What happens in any organisation is effort and cost. To speak of profit centres is, as Drucker put it, 'a polite euphemism'. So the breaking down of the organisation into cost centres, through which the accounting transactions can be sub-divided, helps management to assess the effectiveness and performance of that area again at a given budget. Using cost centre accounting without budgets is rather a pointless exercise, so it is sometimes useful to think of cost centres as budget centres too.

Within Pegasus Senior nominal ledger, a separate code is provided for cost centres, and the nominal accounts can be associated with the various cost centre codes (see Figure 3.2). This avoids the need to duplicate many accounts, since only the cost centre code to which they apply need change. In this respect, it is best to organise your cost centre requirements first. Each sub-division of the organisation that requires separate budget control, or other management and financial reporting, should be identified and assigned a cost centre code. This is a four-character code, and can be used either as a shorthand description of the centre (eg ADMN for administration) or in a more complex format, if you think that further reporting divisions may be beneficial. Once the cost centres are defined, you can begin assigning the nominal accounts that will be appropriate to the various cost centres.

Nominal accounts	Cost centres
Light and heat	Administration
Insurances	
Legal fees	Workshop repairs
Travelling expenses	
Advertising. . .	Retail sales outlet

Table 3.1   Cost Centre to Account Allocation

Notice in Table 3.1 that the concept is that for each cost centre, a set of nominal accounts applies, but only one set of accounts needs to be defined in the first instance.

For users of Single-User nominal ledger, the cost centre code facility is not available, and the same result has to be achieved by use of the nominal code itself, or careful use of the account description. If the description field is used to identify cost centres, then the report generator will need to be used to group the accounts together in the appropriate order, since the nominal ledger programs themselves only sort by account number. Either way, you will need to enter one account for every account and cost centre combination, which means that you will need to enter more account records than a user of the Senior nominal ledger (see Table 3.2).

Account code	Description
A001	ADMIN — Assets
A002	WAREHOUSE — Assets
A003	RETAIL — Assets
H001	ADMIN — Heat and light
H002	WAREHOUSE — Heat and light
H003	RETAIL — Heat and light
etc	

Table 3.2   Single-User Cost Centre Organisation

As Table 3.2 shows, for each cost centre, a corresponding nominal account needs to be set up, so if three cost centres were used, each appropriate profit and loss account would need to be repeated three times. However, there will be some accounts for items that do not apply to the budget control of the individual cost centres, and these would only need to be specified once.

In the example shown, the description begins with the name of the cost centre, followed by the account description itself. Using the report generator, reports could be organised to group together all accounts which had a description beginning with ADMIN, for example. Alternatively, you may choose to use the account code, and in the same example, the last digit of the nominal account code could define the cost centre as 1, 2 or 3 and so on. Again, the report generator allows for accounts to be accumulated under a selected range of account code characters, so that, for example, all accounts whose account code ends in 1 could be selected for a budget variance report.

The important message that should come across is that when designing your account code structures, you should be constantly bearing in mind the potential use of the various fields provided. Chapter 7 covers the use of the report generator in more detail and the facility is probably one of the most important features of the ledgers, after those that deal with the actual recording of transactions.

It is easy to use simple and easy to remember coding structures for the sake of a straightforward time setting up the accounts. The problem with such an approach, which lacks forethought and imagination, is that it only serves to restrict the reporting potential of the software, and wastes the otherwise invaluable information that can be gleaned from the data that lies in the files of the accounting system.

THE SPECIAL REPORT CODE

The production of the final accounts — the profit and loss statement and balance sheet — also requires planning ahead, and can affect the accounts that you define within the nominal ledger. It is not unknown for those of an accounting disposition to set up the designs of the profit and loss and balance sheet reports before setting up any nominal accounts. It is certainly good advice to set out the designs with report code totals before you enter totals in the accounts themselves, however, if you set the parameter option to print these reports before you set up your accounts, you will be prompted for input of a report code at the time you set up an account, and the entry is mandatory. Therefore, if you set up a chart of accounts first, you can either enter any arbitrary report code for each account and amend it later, or set up the accounts with the final accounts option switched off, and set it to Y when you are ready to enter the report codes.

Accounts will either be destined for a profit and loss account or a balance sheet depending upon the nature of the account. The report code for each account will therefore have some indication whether the account is for profit and loss accounting or balance sheet accounting, and this takes the form of a single letter P or B. This code only ever appears in the account header or detail record, however, and is not used on the report designs themselves. This is because when you set up a balance sheet design, for example, the programs already know that any report codes contained in the design will be those prefixed with a B, and likewise with the profit and loss report, those prefixed with a P. Knowing which accounts belong to which report is a matter of book-keeping know-how and an understanding of the nature of accounts in business. If you are not familiar with these procedures, you will probably not use the final accounts reporting facility, but leave your accountants to do this work for you. Even those organisations who do set up final accounts on the Pegasus nominal ledger are well advised to at least seek assistance from their accountants if they are in any way unsure about financial accounting. The following is a guide for the general readership.

The Balance Sheet

This will contain such items as:

Fixed assets:
    land and buildings
    plant and machinery
    furniture and fittings
    patents and rights owned
    motor vehicles, etc
    (less their depreciation)

Current assets:
    stock
    cash in hand
    cash at bank
    debtors (balance of debtors control account)
    etc

Current liabilities:
    creditors (balance of the creditors control account)
    bank overdrafts
    taxation
    dividends
    etc

Financed by:
    share capital
    reserves (profit brought forward)

The format you choose for the balance sheet may be either

'horizontal', with liabilities on the left-hand side and assets on the right; or 'vertical' with two halves, with the top half perhaps for funds and/or capital employed and the bottom half showing net assets employed. The net current assets are arrived at by deducting the current liabilities from the current assets.

The Profit and Loss Statement

This generally comprises the following items:

Sales during the period

less cost of sales

plus other non-trading income

(this provides the gross profit figure)

less expenditure including:
    salaries and wages
    materials bought (not as cost of sales)
    repairs
    advertising
    depreciation costs
    heat and light
    insurances
    office stationery
    packaging
    carriage in and out
    discount given
    etc

(which gives the net profit figure)

The profit value appears on both the profit and loss report and the balance sheet, but is not the balance of a particular account in the nominal ledger. In the case of the profit and loss report, the net profit figure is calculated by adding together all the balances of the nominal accounts which are for profit and loss accounting.

By adding debits and credits together, addition and subtraction takes place (rather like adding plusses and minuses). For example, sales accounts will have a credit balance, whereas expense accounts will have a debit balance. Add the two together and you arrive at a difference between the two.

The profit and loss total is a special report code only used in the report design, and the same code is used in the balance sheet. In the case of the balance sheet, the value of net profit calculated in the profit and loss report is automatically transferred.

Prepayments and accruals have to be catered for and these are balance sheet items. A prepayment is a current asset, since it is money which has been paid in advance. An accrual is a liability, since it represents an amount owing which has accrued. Both are generally included for the purposes of accurate reporting for the period-end as explained previously.

All accounts have to be included somewhere in the reports, since, once the option is set, every account (excluding heading accounts only) must have a special report code, but care must be taken to include all codes in the designs themselves. This is why it is a good idea to plan the report code requirements first using the profit and loss and balance sheet designs, before assigning them to accounts. Trying to do so the other way round tends to make life a little confusing.

In Pegasus Senior, nominal accounts can hold two special report codes: one for the standard ledger, and one for the consolidated ledger, if more than one nominal ledger is to be consolidated. This caters for larger organisations that keep separate nominal ledgers for divisions, subsidiaries or cost centres, and who wish to consolidate the values of these separate ledgers into one group ledger. The design of the profit and loss report and balance sheet for the consolidated ledger is likely to be different from the subsidiary ledger (though it does not have to be), so provision is made for a second report code which identifies where the balance of a particular account is to be accumulated in the consolidated ledger, once the balances have been transferred.

SUSPENSE ACCOUNTS

These are accounts that are used for integration purposes (see also Chapter 6). They are used to hold the value of a transaction which has been transferred from either sales or purchase ledgers because no corresponding nominal ledger account could be found to store the transaction. When this occurs, it is usually due to an invalid analysis code having been used at the time an invoice or credit note was posted. Since these codes are used to determine the resulting nominal account into which the value should be transferred, any anomaly will result in the value being posted to the suspense account automatically. Hence, without a suspense account set up, the programs will not allow any transfers to take place, since it must have this safeguard.

The debtors or creditors control accounts remain the double-entry posting destination for suspense accounts, and a manual journal entry is required to move the amount from suspense into the expense or income account to which it belongs.

Example

Transfer of sales to nominal in which a value of £5,000 has a corresponding analysis code which does not identify a valid nominal account:

	Dr	Cr
Credit the suspense account		£5,000
Debit the debtors control account	£5,000	

To adjust the posting manually therefore:

	Dr	Cr
Debit the suspense account	£5,000	
Credit the income account		£5,000

There is no need to adjust the posting to the debtors control account, since the debit amount would have been posted there in any case.

NOMINAL LEDGER VAT

The way in which you choose to handle VAT in the nominal ledger depends upon your company and the type of business that you operate. For users of the Single-User nominal ledger, who may be using the VAT cash accounting method, reports are provided as part of the system's menu options to cope with reporting on VAT for receipts and payments as opposed to invoices and credit notes.

For those treating VAT under normal methods, the ledger can automatically analyse the VAT elements of invoices and credit notes and transfer these either to one or two accounts in the nominal ledger. Generally, one separates VAT inputs (purchase ledger) and outputs (sales ledger) within the nominal ledger, and the balances of these accounts provide the information which contributes to the VAT return form. However, one could use a consolidated VAT account like the one shown in Figure 3.2.

For VAT return purposes (the Customs and Excise document), the VAT account or accounts should readily provide up-to-date information on the amount of input tax, the amount of output tax, and the amount of VAT owing to Customs and Excise (or in some cases — particularly for exporters — owed by the Customs and Excise). The illustrated account in Figure 3.2, when used on a quarterly basis, will not readily provide this information, as Figure 3.3 shows when a series of postings are included for illustration purposes.

VAT Account (Consolidated)			
Dr			Cr
From Purchase Ledger	4,000	From Sales Ledger	17,000
Payment to HM C & E	13,000		
Account now balances	17,000		17,000

Figure 3.2   Consolidated VAT Account

In Figure 3.3, showing the postings to the consolidated VAT account, the payment of VAT (£1,433.23) would be derived from the following sources of information:

a) looking at the balance of VAT as at 31.05.90, and;

b) accumulating the inputs and outputs for March, April and May.

VAT Account (Consolidated)					
Dr					**Cr**
31.07.90	Purchase Ledger	523.84	01.07.90	Brought Fwd	1726.99
			31.07.90	Sales Ledger	657.76
31.07.90	Balance Carried Forward	1860.91			
		2384.75			2384.75
31.08.90	Purchase Ledger	476.73	01.08.90	Balance B/Fwd	1860.91
31.08.90	Payment of VAT to 31.05	1433.23	31.08.90	Sales Ledger	579.76
31.08.90	Balance Carried Forward	530.71			
		2440.67			2440.67

Figure 3.3   Consolidation VAT Quarterly

This system has the advantage that it only requires one VAT account in the nominal ledger, however, the disadvantage is that it does not provide the necessary information for the VAT form in a readily available format.

Another method of handling the VAT in the nominal ledger is by setting up two VAT accounts; one for inputs (from the purchase ledger), the other for outputs (from the sales ledger). In addition, it will be necessary to set up a VAT control account.

Each month (or period), the inputs and outputs will be posted to the relevant accounts, and the total of each will be the total paid or collected in the current VAT period and not yet payable to Customs and Excise. At the end of the current VAT period (ie at the end of a three-month period), the totals of the two VAT accounts should be posted, by journal entry, to the VAT control account. Figure 3.4 shows an example of this method of handling VAT requirements in the nominal.

VAT Input Account					
Dr					Cr
31.03.90	Purchase Ledger	515.11	31.05.90	To Control VAT	1545.33
30.04.90	Purchase Ledger	485.23			
31.05.90	Purchase Ledger	544.99			
VAT Output Account					
31.05.90	To VAT Control	2978.56	31.03.90	Sales Ledger	978.56
			30.04.90	Sales Ledger	995.78
			31.05.90	Sales Ledger	1004.22
VAT Control Account					
31.05.90	From VAT Input	1545.33	31.05.90	From VAT Out	2978.56
31.05.90	Balance C/Fwd	1433.23			
		2978.26			2978.56
30.06.90	JNL Bank Account	1433.23	01.06.90	Balance B/Fwd	1433.23

Figure 3.4   VAT Control Account Processing

In this way, the VAT control account will, for any given VAT period, show the total VAT input (debit), the total VAT output (credit) and the total VAT due (the balance). When the VAT is paid, the control account should be debited and the bank account credited. This will then reduce the balance of the VAT control account to zero. An example of this is shown in Figure 3.5.

Both these forms of VAT account control apply to Single-User and Senior nominal ledger, but there are differences regarding those companies using VAT cash accounting. For them, the VAT due is based upon the actual value of receipts and payments, and therefore the posting values will be different accordingly.

The purchase and sales ledger VAT analysis reports will break down the value of sales and purchases at various rates of VAT, so that the totals of these can be used to complete the remaining details on the form, regarding the total value of sales and purchases which contribute to VAT input and output. These will need to be accumulated from the three reports for the quarter, unless you are analysing invoice and credit notes by VAT rate within the nominal ledger when a transfer is carried out.

EXCHANGE RATE DISCREPANCIES

Foreign currency accounting requires particular attention to the fluctuation of exchange rates. When an invoice transaction is recorded in either the sales or purchase ledgers, the exchange rate prevailing at the time the invoice was issued is recorded with the transaction. The conversion to the home currency of the foreign value of the invoice can either be based on the exchange held in the company parameters (Pegasus Senior only), or by manual entry at the time the transaction is recorded.

Exchange rates fluctuate regularly, however, and after the invoice is recorded its home currency equivalent can change from day to day. At any stage prior to receiving or making payment for the invoice, the transaction can be revalued to *show* the discrepancies that may exist due to a change in exchange rate (by discrepancy, we mean profit (gain) or loss on conversion). For example:

02.05.90   Invoice   SFr 2 440,00

Exchange rate at time of posting: 2.640

Home currency equivalent on 02.05.90:   £924.24

20.05.90 exchange rate changed to: 2.531

Home currency equivalent on 20.05.90   £964.04

Exchange discrepancy (gain)   £39.80

The *actual* exchange discrepancy is not realised, however, until a receipt or payment is made in respect of the invoice and the amount, after conversion at the prevailing exchange rate, is calculated. Consequently, any foreign currency transaction is likely to lead to a corresponding exchange discrepancy when the transaction is honoured.

The Senior nominal ledger provides a facility for discrepancy reporting. This allows reporting on all accounts or *potential* discrepancies which are almost certain to have arisen.

It is not always possible to wait until all invoices are paid before one assesses the gain or loss on transactions. If a company processes large numbers of foreign invoices, the profit and loss and balance sheet for the period will only reflect the value of the invoices at the time they were posted, unless some adjustments are made to compensate for possible gains or losses. These discrepancies can amount to very large sums of money indeed, and it is therefore important to acknowledge them.

This requires the revaluation of outstanding amounts and the posting of a journal entry to compensate. How often revaluation takes place depends on how important it is to realise the current gains or losses being made. Generally, it is required for balance sheet purposes, since the value of foreign transactions affects both the debtors (current assets) and creditors (liabilities) totals.

The nominal ledger therefore includes a facility for posting reported discrepancies by means of automatic journal entries. The discrepancies are posted to the appropriate exchange adjustment account.

4 The Sales Ledger

The sales ledger records the information that relates to the transactions you make with your customers. For each customer you deal with, at least on a regular basis, you will keep a record of who they are, and what transactions have been undertaken in doing business with them. Basically, you need to record the customer name and address and then make an entry on their account each time a transaction involving money is made. It is important to store such information for two reasons. Firstly, you are required, by law, to keep a record of your business transactions so that they can be accounted for, for tax purposes. Secondly, and particularly if you have many customers, you need to know who owes you money if, as in most circumstances, you give your customers credit, ie they do not pay for their goods immediately.

The Pegasus sales ledger provides for more information to be stored about your customers other than simply their names and addresses. Other details can be useful when dealing with customers on a regular basis, for example a contact name and/or telephone number, and some items stored with your customer records in a Pegasus sales ledger relate to the way in which you deal with that customer. For example, you may impose a credit limit on an account which dictates the maximum amount that you will allow that customer to owe you at any one time.

Sales ledger transactions can generally be categorised under one of the following headings:

— invoices;

— credit notes;

— receipts;

— refunds;

— adjustments.

For those readers who are new to accounting principles with respect to a sales ledger, the above transaction types are briefly explained in the following paragraphs.

A sales ledger invoice records a sales transaction when you sell your goods or services to a customer. For example, when you sell goods for £1,200 to a customer, you will raise an invoice for that amount, and record it as a transaction on your sales ledger in the appropriate customer account. Unless that customer pays for those goods immediately, the invoice is a debt as far as the customer is concerned. We therefore refer to customers who owe us money as debtors. When the customer pays for the goods, you record a receipt transaction on the ledger, and, if the customer pays the full amount of the invoice, the debt is cleared.

There are occasions when, having raised an invoice for a customer, you need to cancel all or part of it as a result of, for example, the return of some goods by the customer that were damaged. In such cases, you raise a credit note for the customer and record this transaction on the customer's account. A credit note is like the opposite of an invoice, it gives the customer credit to a value which corresponds either to all or part of a previously raised invoice.

If payment has been received for goods that are returned or credited, you may, in certain circumstances, provide a refund of the money, rather than allowing credit against any future sales.

Adjustments to the account sometimes need to be made when the account balance needs to be amended for some other purpose than previously mentioned. For example, you may decide to write off an amount which is not likely to be paid, particularly if it is a very small amount, and you wish to tidy up the account. Adjustments may also be made if you suspect a bad debt, and the outstanding invoice transactions on the accounts are defaulted by the customer concerned.

The Pegasus sales ledger provides for all of these transaction requirements. Once you are storing your day-to-day sales, then you can obtain lists of data to help you manage your customer accounts. These reports (sometimes referred to as audit trails) are the result of the software program searching through all the customer records and listing details in order to provide an overall picture of the status of the sales ledger. The reports range from a list of customer details for reference purposes, through lists of invoices, credit notes, receipts, refunds and adjustments posted to the accounts, to more important reports such as statements, which you can send to your customers to show the status of their account, and listings that show the amounts each customer owes you and for how long transactions have been outstanding.

The sales ledger, then, records the details of sales transactions made between you and the customers. You should remember that when we refer to 'sales' we mean only the sales of goods or services which relate to normal business transactions, and not the sales of assets, income received from royalties and other forms of non-trading income.

TRANSACTIONS

The ledger processing functions allow transactions to be added to the account. These are dealt with in one of two ways: open item or balance forward accounting. Open item accounting ensures that transactions remain as separate outstanding transactions with full details, until such time as they are cleared from the accounts because they are satisfied one way or another. Balance forward only shows current period transactions in this way: at the end of the period, all outstanding transactions that are one or more periods old are combined into brought forward balances for each period in which there are outstanding amounts.

This balance forward method serves to reduce the amount of disk space used for storing transactions, since the disk space required for a single balance value is far less than a series of transactions. Apart from this advantage, there are few, if any, other reasons for using this method of accounting. The account record carries an indication of the method in which transactions are to be treated, and it is quite possible to mix accounts using balance forward processing alongside those that use open item in the same sales ledger.

Open item transaction processing relies on a method of allocating debits and credits. When an invoice is posted to an account, the transaction shows the outstanding balance, aged according to the date of the transaction. Allocation (also referred to as 'matching') enables a receipt to be marked as allocated to the corresponding invoice, and the invoice is likewise marked as paid. If only part payment is recorded, then the invoice retains an outstanding balance to be allocated on another occasion. The month-end procedure is responsible for clearing fully allocated transactions from the accounts. Thus, if in the month of April, the account's status is as follows:

15.03.90	Invoice	Paid	1240.57	
20.04.90	Receipt	Alloc		1240.57
23.04.90	Invoice		231.76	

then after the month-end procedure, the paid and allocated items will be removed, so that the account's status at the beginning of May stands at:

23.04.90	Invoice	231.76

and the amount outstanding will be aged so that it appears in the '1 month old' field of the account.

Credit notes, receipts and negative adjustments can all be allocated to invoices, and the procedure for allocation can either be carried out at the time a receipt is posted, or as a separate routine altogether. Receipts that are posted to the accounts but not allocated are called 'cash on account' receipts and require separate allocation to outstanding amounts before they are cleared from the accounts.

All transactions that are visible on an account (for example, through the enquiry routine) will appear on the customer's statement when printed. This shows exactly what transactions have been processed during any given period, but can be rather embarrassing if the account is full of adjustments and mispostings, even though the balance may be correct. It is worth knowing, therefore, that you can suppress the printing of statements for selected accounts by placing an asterisk in the account's comment box.

When used with other Pegasus modules, such as invoicing and sales order processing or retail accounting, the transactions recorded on the sales ledger are not necessarily entered through the ledger processing functions. The ledger processing transaction entry routines are a manual processing function, and for integrated systems, where Pegasus invoicing raises all the appropriate invoice transactions, ledger processing will tend to be used for adjustments and receipt processing only.

If invoices are entered manually, then there is no batch total checking for occasions when many invoices are entered on several accounts in one procedure. However, you can make use of the debtors total display screen for this purpose. This enquiry, available from the ledger processing menu, displays the total of outstanding debts on the sales ledger (see Figure 4.1).

By recording this figure prior to posting transactions, and adding up all the invoice totals in the batch, you can compare, after posting the invoices, the change in debtors total with your batch total. If the two agree, then you know that no invoices have been missed in the batch input procedure. The same trick can be used for the batch posting of cheques.

Pegasus Senior provides a facility for defining descriptions of receipts and adjustments. These are used to break down an analysis of these transactions under various headings. For example, you may wish to separate the receipt totals for different payment methods, such as cash, cheque, credit card, etc. The list of receipts and adjustments will then total the various amounts under their corresponding headings. Any receipts and adjustments with any other description are grouped under a sundry heading.

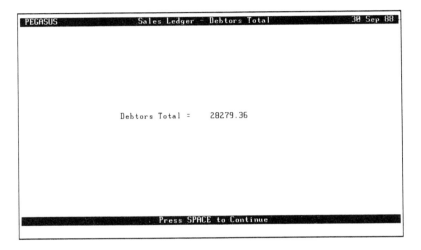

Figure 4.1   Debtors Total for Batch Checking

Advance Posting Transactions

Pegasus Senior sales ledger provides what is described as an advance posting facility. This enables transactions to be posted which actually belong to the next period's accounts. The reason for needing such a facility arises when approaching the month-end, and not all the current month's transactions have been completed. As the beginning of the new month arrives and still transactions remain outstanding on the ledger, but invoices are already being raised in the new period, the new invoices can be posted as 'advanced'. The effect of this is that they will be displayed on the account in the normal way (with an indicator of 'ADV') but when the month-end procedure is actually carried out, any transactions in the advanced status are retained for the new period's analysis file (the month-end procedure removes the analysis file of the sales ledger for all non-advanced transactions). See Figure 4.2 for a diagrammatical example.

Analysis file before month-end procedure:

20-04-90   April Analysis Transaction 1
28-04-90   April Analysis Transaction 2
30-04-90   April Analysis Transaction 3
02-05-90   April Analysis Transaction 4
05-05-90   April Analysis Transaction 5
06-05-90   May (Advance Posting) Analysis Transaction 6
07-05-90   April Analysis Transaction 7
07-05-90   May (Advance Posting) Analysis Transaction 8

08-05-90   April's month-end procedure carried out

Analysis file after month-end procedure:

06-05-90   May Analysis Transaction 1
07-05-90   May Analysis Transaction 2

Figure 4.2   Advanced Postings

CREDIT CONTROL

The most important business function of a sales ledger is the control of outstanding debts. It is important for ensuring good cash flow control, and therefore making optimum use of financial assets. Most sales ledgers provide a degree of credit control which is adequate for tracing all outstanding amounts, and the advantage over any manual accounting system is the speed with which such information can be obtained from the accounts.

The tracking of outstanding debts within the Pegasus sales ledgers is provided by the following routines:

— account enquiries;

— debtors total enquiry;

— aged debtors list;

— statements;

— debtors letter facility.

Aged Debts

Transactions are automatically analysed across accounting periods (usually monthly) so that the age of a debt can be ascertained quickly. An account enquiry will report the status of aged debts for the particular account concerned. If using foreign currency accounting within Pegasus Senior, then outstanding debts are shown in both the home and foreign currency equivalents.

The aged debtors listing is particularly useful since it indicates, at a glance, slow paying customers, as well as those who have exceeded their credit limit, and gives totals (and optionally subtotals if the appropriate parameter option is set) of the amounts of debt outstanding for each accounting period from the current period to three months and older. This report should be printed out towards the end of the month or near the time you would normally send statements. It helps identify priorities for chasing particular customers who have long-outstanding debts, and to whom you way wish to send a reminder letter.

Reminder letters are a useful backup to statements. Some organisations work on the basis of sending one statement, followed by reminder letters, others send regular repeat statements. If you choose to send a reminder letter, then the sales ledger provides a facility for automatically printing preworded letters for accounts that have balances which exceed a predefined number of days. For example, you could print a reminder for all accounts that have debts over 60 days old. The program selects the account for inclusion in the print run on the basis that it has debts with a transaction date that is more than 60 days from the current system date. The letters can include details of the account transactions involved, by using special codes which instruct the program to insert the appropriate transaction information in a certain place in the text of the letter, thus making it look like an individually produced reminder. Up to three levels of reminder letter can be set up, each one for a different period of time over which a debt may be outstanding, and therefore with text that may be progressively more terse the older the debt. Figure 4.3 shows an example debtors letter printout.

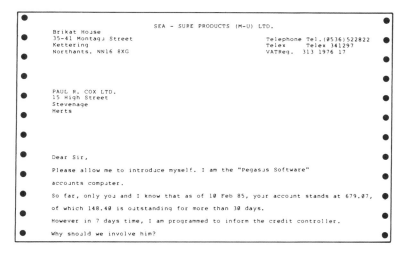

Figure 4.3   Example Debtors Letter

Another form of credit control is the use of interest calculation on outstanding amounts. Pegasus Single-User provides an optional facility which allows you to enter a percentage of interest that may be applied to a customer account, and a period number field which indicates how many periods a transaction must be overdue before any interest is calculated. There are various implications for charging interest on overdue accounts and these are adequately documented in the sales ledger manual in an appendix. Using interest is not a common practice in the United Kingdom, and there are few companies who would acknowledge an interest payment under normal circumstances. However, the effectiveness of such a credit control measure is probably best realised by informing your customers of the fact that interest is chargeable, thereby using the facility more as a deterrent against slow payment. The 'opposite' approach to charging interest, and the more common method used is offering settlement discount, as mentioned in the paragraphs below.

GIVING CUSTOMERS DISCOUNT

In book-keeping terms, this is what is known as *discount allowed* or *discount given*. There are a number of reasons why you might want to give a customer discount on the invoice value of goods or services sold:

— the customer is regular and warrants discount on the basis that you value the continued business and wish to maintain it;

— the customer is entitled to a lower price than the normal retail value where such goods are resold. In these cases, discount should more accurately be described as the resale margin or trade discount;

— you wish to encourage the customer to pay the account promptly, so you will accept a lower amount of payment for an invoice if paid within a specified period of time. This is known as either cash discount or settlement discount;

— you give discount to a customer who purchases more than a certain number or amount of goods, thereby encouraging orders for larger quantities.

Discounts are recorded on the sales ledger at the time a receipt is posted, with the amount of discount entered in the 'VAT or Disc' field on the posting routine screen. This value, plus the actual cheque or receipt amount, together reflect the total of the invoice transaction, and therefore all three transactions can be allocated.

Discount amounts are analysed to the nominal ledger (if integrated) to the discount allowed or discount given account, with a double-entry posting to the debtors control account, just as if it were a receipt. The discount itself is actually an expense item, since it is a *cost* to the company that reduces its prices.

The Senior sales ledger account name and address update routine has additional boxes to its Single-User counterpart for the recording of discounts associated with various customers, though these are used for integration to the invoicing and order processing modules, and are not used to calculate discount on the invoice of a manually posted transaction. The programs will, however, check the amount of settlement discount entitlement associated with an account and inform the operator if the amount of discount taken seems disproportionate to the entitlement, and this includes checking whether the transaction falls within the settlement discount period.

ANALYSING INVOICES

As a preamble to the chapter on analysis facilities, this section describes how invoices and credit notes are broken down into analysis values when posted to the ledger. For each invoice value posted to an account, the net value (ie the goods value without VAT) can be further analysed or broken down into between 1 and 10 separate values. Invoices may often be for more than one goods item, and the analysis facility enables each section of the invoice to be grouped into various divisions. For example, suppose an invoice was raised for the following goods:

Description	Qty	Unit	Value
'Executive' chairs	2	89.50	179.00
Copy holder	1	38.00	38.00
Labels (rolls 200)	3	4.20	12.60
Total goods value			229.60

The three items on the invoice may be analysed to just one total for sundry office supplies (the full 229.60). On the other hand, if a detailed analysis is required of the items sold either through the sales ledger's own analysis facility, or for integration to the nominal ledger, then one might break the invoice down into the three values shown. For nominal integration purposes, for example, it may be pertinent to analyse the value of the labels to a packaging sales account, the chairs to a furniture sales account, and the copy holder to office supplies sales.

However invoices and credit notes are analysed, the total of all the analysis value items must equal the goods total of the invoice before the transaction is accepted for processing. Pegasus Senior permits the analysis to be based not only on an analysis code, but also by quantity, so you can analyse the quantity sales of individually invoiced items. When integrated to the invoicing module, the analysis breakdown occurs automatically according to each line of the invoice. Where ten analysis lines are insufficient to analyse lengthy invoices, the use of the invoicing module will be the answer.

For each analysis line of an invoice transaction, a corresponding entry is made in the sales ledger analysis file. It is this file which is responsible for providing all the user-definable sales analysis reports *and* the source of information for integration to the nominal ledger.

The analysis may optionally include an analysis of VAT rate amounts. This permits analysis values to be analysed according to the rate of VAT applicable. For example, an invoice which includes books and gift items would have two rates of VAT applicable (at least under current legislation) — the values of the books would be analysed at zero rate VAT, since VAT does not apply, whereas the gift items would be subject to the standard rate of VAT. The analysis codes for the VAT rates are entered alongside the analysis value column and this forms the basis for a VAT analysis report, which is provided as a standard option on the sales ledger analysis menu (see Figure 4.4).

Information on the sales of goods by VAT rate code helps

provide the statistical information required by the VAT return form, which requires the total of sales attributable to the VAT inputs amount.

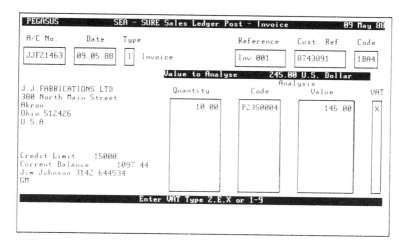

Figure 4.4   VAT Analysis

SALES TURNOVER

As invoices are posted to the customer accounts, the system maintains a turnover total for each one. This figure is net of VAT and can be a useful piece of information about your customers and the level of business that they do with you. The month-end routine provides the means to clear this turnover amount so that it always reflects the turnover for the month-to-date. If left uncleared, then it accumulates the turnover throughout the year. Adjustments and other sundry postings do not affect the turnover figure, however, and there is a tendency for users of Pegasus, when first setting up opening balances on customer accounts at the start of their processing, to use adjustment transactions to do so.

The disadvantage is clearly that the opening balance will not be reflected in the turnover amount. Only invoice transactions increment the turnover field. Thoughtful use of the turnover field by using the report generator facility can put this information to use.

For one thing, there is no turnover report as a standard menu option, but the report generator can be used to extract turnovers for a range of accounts, perhaps all those over a certain value, which indicate your 'top ten' customers (see Chapter 7 for more information about the report generator).

An extension of the use of this field might be to control an incentive campaign to increase sales. For example, if you use the month-end procedure to clear all turnover figures, then, based on previous levels of business, you could set new sales targets for customers for an incentive, such as discounted goods, a prize or other temptation, and the turnover field can be used to measure performance against the targets. Similarly, the field may be used to measure internal incentives and sales performance figures associated with a sales force, and to indicate increased business levels on which commission payments may be based.

DAY-TO-DAY SALES LEDGER PROCESSING

The following documents the typical day-to-day procedures that one might encounter when operating the sales ledger. Of course, the actual procedures will vary from company to company, but for those not familiar with sales ledger processing, the following offers an overview of the processing involved.

Sorting the Post

At the start of each day's processing, invoices ready for despatch (or copies of invoices already sent) and receipts that have arrived in the post relating to customer accounts need to be sorted for transaction posting. Any new accounts not already stored on the ledger should be put at the top of the pile. You may find it useful to allocate analysis codes and other static information relating to the new accounts prior to posting. As a minimum, you will need to know:

— the account number to be allocated to the customer;

— the account name and address;

— the account analysis code;

— whether the account is open item or balance forward;

— the currency code, if the account is foreign.

All other details are optional, and it is up to you whether you enter them at this stage or add them later. For both invoices and receipts, total up all the amounts to provide a batch total. In the case of invoices, this should be including VAT.

You may wish to allocate analysis codes to the invoices before they are posted on the ledger, if they are not apparent to the operator. This will save time when the postings are actually made. If the number of analysis codes is a manageable size, some companies provide operators with a quick reference list of analysis codes from which they can select at the time of posting.

Account Name Update

If any new customer accounts are to be added, set these up first. You cannot create new accounts at the same time as posting the first transaction for the account as all posting routines require the account to be set up already.

Also check for changes of address or other details relating to an account that may have been notified, and include these changes as part of the update procedure. Print a new list of accounts if there have been additions and/or amendments, and replace your existing copy with the new one.

Batch Check

If you wish to carry out a batch check, as described previously, call up the screen which displays the debtors total and make a note of this amount. Add to this figure the total of all invoices to be posted and record that figure. Then deduct the total of all receipts and record this figure also. These will be needed later, so keep them by the machine.

Senior Company Parameters

If foreign currency processing, make sure that the exchange rate file is up-to-date with today's currency rates, otherwise make individual checks when posting foreign invoices as mentioned below.

Invoice Posting

Post the day's invoices to the appropriate accounts. Make sure that the VAT is recorded accurately — Pegasus sales ledger does not calculate this and only checks that it is not a disproportionate figure. If posting invoices to foreign accounts, check the latest exchange rate is correct.

Double check the analysis codes (if using Single-User). Senior programs will automatically check for the existence of the nominal ledger account to which the analysis value will ultimately be posted.

If any account posting causes the customer's credit limit to be exceeded, put the invoice to one side for query, and cancel the posting by pressing the escape key, unless you are sure that the posting of the invoice is acceptable. Similarly, put aside invoices for any accounts that are on stop.

Mark on the invoice, in some easily identifiable way, the fact that it has been posted to the ledger (you can get ready made rubber stamps with the word 'Posted' and perhaps a date, for this purpose). When all invoices (and credit notes) have been added to the file, print a list of invoices and credit notes.

If batch checking, call up the debtors total again to see if the total matches your addition of the previous total plus the invoices. Do not forget to subtract any invoices that were not posted because the account was on stop or the credit limit was exceeded.

If the batch totals still do not agree, check through the invoices for those not entered or entered incorrectly.

Posting Receipts

You may wish to separate those receipts that can be allocated to outstanding invoices from those that will be posted as cash on account before you begin.

Add the receipts to the appropriate accounts. Do not forget to take into account any discount that may have been taken, and enter this in the discount field of the ledger posting.

When allocating receipts, take care to ensure that you are allocating the correct transactions, or in the case of balance forward accounts, to the right period number.

When all receipts have been added to the ledger, print a list of receipts and adjustments. If batch checking, call up the debtors total screen again to see whether the total displayed matches your previously recorded total after receipts.

Adjustments

If any adjustments need to be made to accounts, carry these out before printing the list of receipts and adjustments. Adjustments may be needed to write off odd small amounts on accounts, record bad debts, misposts, etc.

Finally, take a backup of your data files at the end of the current processing.

PERIOD PROCESSING

On a period basis, you will also need to perform the following procedures:

- print an aged debtors report to check on outstanding amounts;

— print statements at the end of the month, or the start of a new month, for all customers with outstanding balances;

— for those accounts that have been identified as having particularly old debts, run the debt collection letters routine;

— before carrying out a month-end procedure, make sure that you have printed the sales analysis reports that are needed. Once the month-end procedure has been carried out, the analysis file will have been removed. Also ensure that the invoices and credit notes, receipts and adjustments have been posted to the nominal ledger;

— for foreign currency processing, print a currency discrepancy report. This includes all outstanding transactions for foreign currency accounts and will show the original foreign currency value at the time a transaction was posted, the original home value, the new home currency revalued with the latest exchange rate and the loss or gain on the conversion.

PERIOD-END ROUTINE

Once all the processing has been carried out for the period, the period-end (month-end) routine can be carried out. Make sure you take backups of your data files before you do this.

When you choose the period-end routine, in the case of Pegasus Senior, the programs will check whether the option has been set in the parameters for integration to the nominal ledger. If so, and the transfer routines have not been carried out, the program will inform the operator that the transfer has not been completed, and the routine will not be permitted to proceed.

All analysis reports must be printed before the month-end is carried out, otherwise the data contained in the analysis files will go unreported.

You can optionally clear the account turnovers as part of the month-end procedure, or leave them to accumulate over the year. On Pegasus Senior sales ledgers, a further prompt will ask whether all disputed markers are to be removed. These are transaction 'flags' which indicate that an invoice, for example, is in dispute. The program will clear all such markers if this is required.

Once the procedure begins, the programs will create a set of temporary working files. Into these files, the program will reorganise accounts into account number order, removing all accounts that have been marked for deletion and, if the appropriate parameter option is set, all accounts with zero balances.

All paid and allocated items are removed and balance forward accounts have their period transactions consolidated into a balance forward figure. All advance postings become 'current' and their information is added to the new analysis file. The old analysis file is cleared.

FURTHER DETAILS

The differences between the Pegasus Senior and Single-User sales ledgers are quite significant. Appendix A shows a list of the main variances, though not all. Basically, however, the function of the sales ledger remains the same; both provide detailed information about the transactions that are recorded when doing business with customers.

For those organisations that mainly deal in retailing, and therefore predominantly cash customers, the sales ledger does not offer the right transaction processing procedures. Pegasus produces a separate retail accounting module for this purpose which integrates with the sales ledger. In this case, the sales ledger holds the cash accounts, and any credit accounts, while the retail accounting module provides the transaction processing, optionally linked to a stock control. The cash transactions are still stored in the sales ledger, and can be transferred to the nominal ledger accordingly.

For users of Pegasus Senior, an associated module for sales ledger is the sales history module. This provides a means of analysing sales transactions over many periods, rather than the one period which the standard sales analysis provides. It only works in conjunction with the sales ledger, and reads the necessary period information, accumulating analysis values for reporting over various periods of time. This enables trends of sales to be seen clearly, showing variations in both market and individual customer's business.

5 The Purchase Ledger

The Pegasus purchase ledger is the focal point for the recording of purchases on credit, consisting of accounts relating to each supplier and the transactions that take place between them and the company. As with most computerised purchase ledgers, the function of the system mirrors the sales ledger module closely. Accounts and transactions are recorded in a similar way, except that the resulting postings relate to expenditure rather than income.

Each time a credit purchase is made from a supplier, an invoice is generally sent detailing the goods or services bought and the terms under which they are due for payment. The invoice is recorded on the purchase ledger, and when the invoice is due, a payment recorded and posted.

Pegasus purchase ledger provides a number of features which help to keep track of the invoices outstanding with suppliers, and particularly useful functions for payment processing. The essence of controlling the purchases of a company is to ensure that, while satisfying the cash flow requirements of the organisation as far as possible (which for some companies simply means avoiding payment for as long as possible), settlement discounts are taken advantage of, and, in the case of foreign currency transactions, payments are made at the most advantageous exchange rates.

To make this level of management control possible, information is needed about outstanding transactions, how old they are, when they are due, what discount entitlements are available and the current value of transactions in the home currency. Pegasus purchase ledger includes a number of reports that make this information available, and the report generator (described in Chapter 7) can extend this reporting capability further still.

There are no facilities for recording purchase orders on the purchase ledger, but such a facility is provided within the Pegasus stock control system, and the Senior purchase ledger account records hold the balance (value) of current orders which have been raised against any particular supplier. The functions of purchase ledger are concentrated on invoice and payment processing.

TERMS OF PAYMENT

Invoices sent from suppliers usually state the normal terms of business. This will indicate the length of time that is allowed (the credit given) before the invoice is due for payment. Each supplier account on the purchase ledger allows the recording of the standard terms of business for the supplier concerned. This is expressed in a number of days before payment is due. Most companies operate on the basis of allowing 30 days (1 month) credit, which is effective from the date of the invoice. Hence, an invoice dated 14th December will be due for payment in mid-January. This information is used by the programs in both the suggested and automatic payment routines to deal with the payment of due accounts.

In addition to the normal terms of business, many suppliers offer settlement discount terms to encourage prompt payment, where discount may be taken on the value of the invoice. Again, the suggested and automatic payment routines of the ledger will take this discount into account to ensure you optimise on taking the discounts given.

Using the information provided in the supplier accounts about due invoices, you can quickly see when particular invoices fall due, and this information can be used to assist in the forecasting of your company's cash flow — assessing what outgoings will be required at a given time (the aged creditors list also helps in this respect.)

TRANSACTIONS

The transactions recorded in the purchase ledger are as follows:

— invoices;

— credit notes;

— payments;

— adjustments;

— discounts.

Posting Invoices

Invoices are recorded on the purchase ledger either as they are received or in a batch at an appropriate point during the period. The transaction date stored with the invoice transaction should be the date on the invoice, not the day it is entered. This is because the invoice date is used to establish the due date for payment, and this is normally based on the terms of payment from the invoice date.

The correct use of the reference field is something that needs careful consideration when using Single-User purchase ledger. Only one reference field is provided of up to ten characters. This means that it is usually used to record the supplier's invoice number, so that should any queries arise in connection with the transaction, an account enquiry can be displayed showing the supplier invoice numbers for easy location. However, many organisations operate an internal referencing system for purchase invoices, often sequential, which assists in the filing of invoices and their subsequent retrieval. The reference may also be required as an order number field. With only one reference field, you will probably need to decide on one or the other.

Users of Senior purchase ledger, on the other hand, have two reference fields, one of which is for the supplier's reference (the purchase invoice number), so that the other may be used for internal referencing purposes. As further assistance in this direction, the reference field will be automatically incremented by 1 each time a new invoice is posted, provided that the first reference used uses at least the last three characters as a numeric entry.

For example, if a reference of SR00013 is used as the first reference on an invoice posting, then the next invoice that is posted (regardless of the account) is automatically offered the reference SR00014, and so on. If the last three characters of the reference are not numeric, then the system will simply display the last reference used as a prompt for the next reference.

The value of the invoice transaction posting is the value including VAT, and the VAT portion of the transaction is entered in the box marked 'VAT or Disc'. You may wish to check the VAT calculation on a purchase invoice prior to posting, to make sure that it is correct before a transaction is created. Remember, however, that if the invoice includes an amount of settlement discount, then the VAT amount should be calculated on the basis of the goods value less settlement discount, so the following formula applies in the case of a standard rate of 15% VAT:

VAT amount = (goods value − amount of discount) x 0.15

In other words, it is assumed that the settlement discount will be taken, so that no further VAT adjustment is required.

When a purchase invoice is subsequently transferred to the nominal ledger accounts, the entries that are made are as follows:

— credit the creditors control account;

— debit the expenditure account.

Where VAT is involved, additional postings are made with respect to the VAT output account, thus:

— credit the creditors control account;

— debit the VAT output account.

The creditors control account always reflects the total amount of money outstanding with suppliers.

Payment Postings

Payments can be posted to the purchase ledger in one of two ways: either by manually entering the posting through the ledger processing option, or by using the automatic payment routine which will generate a payment transaction for each outstanding and due transaction within the range of dates specified.

If manually posting a payment, there are two types that can be made — an allocated payment (ie one that relates to one or more specific invoices) or an unallocated payment, referred to as cash on account. If the payment is the allocated type, then once the payment details have been recorded, a list of outstanding invoice transactions will be displayed against which the payment may be allocated. Items allocated in this way can then be cleared from the accounts, in much the same way as sales ledger transactions.

When posting payments in Senior purchase ledger, a parameter option setting permits the allocation of a particular nominal bank account to which the posting is recorded. In the case of Single-User purchase ledger, all payments are posted to the same bank account specified in the nominal ledger parameters.

The subsequent postings made to the nominal ledger, when the payment is recorded, are as follows:

— debit the creditors control account;

— credit the bank account.

and where discount is involved in the payment, the following postings are also made:

— debit the creditors control account;

— credit the discount taken account.

If the payment is for a foreign currency account, then there may be an exchange discrepancy as a result of a difference in the value of the transaction at the time the corresponding invoice was posted and the present time. In this case, an exchange discrepancy posting is made to the nominal ledger exchange difference account, according to whether a gain or loss has been made on the transaction.

Adjustment Postings

Adjustments are posted to amend the balance of the account according to unusual circumstances, such as the write off of an amount, the correction of a transaction amount, the handling of a misposted amount, etc.

The important thing to remember about adjustment transactions is that they do not affect the purchase analysis files. Unlike invoices and credit notes, which update the analysis file and are therefore transferred to appropriate nominal accounts, adjustments are not analysed in this way and are automatically posted to the suspense account thus:

— debit or credit the creditors suspense account;

— debit or credit the creditors control account.

whether the adjustment posting is recorded as a debit or credit will depend upon the nature of the adjustment, and therefore whether the adjustment value is positive or negative. To move the adjustment to the correct nominal ledger account, a manual journal entry posting will be required in the nominal ledger. For example:

— credit the creditors suspense account;

— debit the expenditure or purchase account.

Adjustments are sometimes used as a means of posting opening balances to purchase accounts when the ledger is first set up. This method is quite satisfactory, provided that you understand that the analysis files will not be updated. This fact is perhaps more important if an adjustment is used to remove an invoice that has been posted to the wrong account. By using an adjustment on the two accounts involved in a 'contra' posting the account balances can be properly adjusted. However, because the account's analysis code is used as part of the analysis file entry, the analysis itself will remain incorrect. This need not be a problem, so long as it is remembered when the analysis reports are printed. The better option for dealing with misposts is to produce a credit note transaction in the one account, and repeat the invoice in the correct account.

INVOICE ANALYSIS

The purchase ledger invoice analysis facility works in a very similar way to the sales ledger with the following exceptions. In addition to the analysis code entries for each line of an invoice that is analysed, a comment field is also available. This does not appear on the purchase analysis reports, but is shown on the nominal ledger transfer report produced when the purchase invoices and credit notes are integrated to the nominal accounts. It helps identify the item or group of items being analysed.

The purchase ledger may be integrated to the Pegasus job costing module, which is used to record the costs incurred in completing a job of work, such as a building project, print publication job, manufacturing process, etc. If the integration is in operation, the invoice analysis in the purchase ledger is extended to allow for the input of job and cost codes, and as such will probably dictate the way in which supplier invoices are analysed. For any one invoice up to ten analysis lines are available, so invoices that require breaking down into more divisions than this either have to be split into more than one transaction or, more usually, the items are grouped under similar expense types as far as possible.

An example purchase invoice analysis screen is shown in Figure

5.1. Note that the far right column is used for VAT analysis purposes, the same as with sales invoices. This enables suppliers with different rates of VAT to be analysed, and the resulting analysis report can, when accumulated over a VAT quarter, be used to provide statistical information for the completion of the VAT return form.

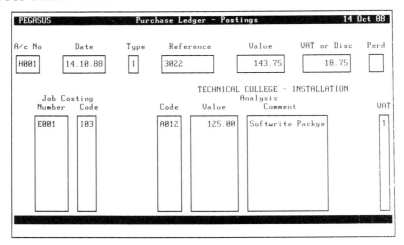

Figure 5.1   Purchase Invoice Analysis

PAYMENT CONTROL

The purchase ledger provides special facilities for payment control of outstanding and due transactions. They take the form of two functions in particular:

— the suggested payments list;

— the automatic payment routine.

The suggested payments facility is a report option which checks through the transactions in the purchase ledger, compares their respective due dates and looks for any settlement discount entitlements. The report literally suggests which transactions should be paid, in order to capitalise on the settlement discounts that are available and to indicate which transactions are due for payment. The content of this report is based upon the selection of transactions up to, but excluding, a given date. It takes into consideration any days-before-payment information entered on the supplier's account and will calculate the amount of settlement discount, advising how much payment is due in total on each account selected. If a transaction is marked as being disputed, it will be ignored.

This list can be used on its own as a prompt for manual payment entries, or to simply list which invoices are offering settlement discount. However, it also serves as a report on the transactions that will be paid by the automatic payment routine, since that routine makes selections on the same criteria.

The automatic payment routine actually generates payment transactions. At the same time, if the account involved is open item, the payment will be allocated to the outstanding transaction or transactions. On Single-User purchase ledger, all transactions generated by the automatic payment routine use the reference 'CHQ', which indicates that the payment can have a corresponding cheque printed for the account. In the case of Senior purchase ledger, payments marked against the transaction have no reference at this stage.

Here's what the automatic payment routine actually does: the operator first enters a pay date and any invoices which are older than, but not including, this date will be included in the payment run. The system calculates and records the days-before-payment information and settlement discount, taking into account credit notes and cash on account, and ignoring foreign currency accounts, advance postings and disputed items.

Once the automatic payment routine has taken place, the option can be taken to print cheques for each account included in the payment run. In the case of Single-User, this will be all payments that have the reference 'CHQ', including any transactions that were manually given this reference. In the case of Senior, all automatically paid and manually marked transactions are included. A start cheque number is prompted for so that the program knows what cheque number reference to assign to each payment record. The cheque number must correspond with that on your cheque stationery, and is incremented by one for each cheque.

Some users are disturbed by the thought of a routine that automatically makes payments 'across the board', but a facility for marking invoices as 'disputed' ensures that those transactions not to be included in the automatic payment routine are omitted. Even worse, however, is the fear of automatically printed cheques being produced based on the automatic payment routine, but to ease the fears of those users not yet convinced that this is a good idea, remember that there is an upper cheque limit parameter which ensures that only those cheques up to that limit are printed, and those amounts that exceed the limit are ignored.

Secondly, the printing out of a cheque does not mean that it is also signed and has to be sent out straight away. Indeed, many companies (in the interests of improving their own cash flow while annoying their suppliers) print the cheques based on an automatic payment routine at the end of every month. Then the cheques are held back until the supplier makes final demands for the account to be settled, at which point the cheque is signed and despatched (probably considerably overdue). This ensures that the settlement discount amount is still taken before the cheque is printed and that the accounts are kept tidy.

REMITTANCE ADVICES

The purchase ledger can print remittance advices for payments that have been recorded on the ledgers. These documents detail the payments made and the transactions to which they relate, and the documents are sent to the suppliers with the cheques. The suppliers, on receiving the remittance advices, can then see exactly what has been paid and update their own accounts.

Within the Single-User purchase ledger, this remittance document has a fixed format and relies upon preprinted stationery

supplied by Pegasus dealers or Pegasus Supplies Limited, a
subsidiary company which produces all standard Pegasus forms. In
the case of Senior purchase ledger, the remittance advice design is
free format, meaning that it can be tailored to fit any stationery,
preprinted or otherwise. Figure 5.2 shows an example remittance
advice output with details of a payment.

Figure 5.2   Remittance Advice

DAY-TO-DAY/AD HOC PURCHASE PROCESSING

The following documents the typical day-to-day procedures that
one might encounter when operating the purchase ledger. As with
sales ledger procedures, these will vary from one organisation to
another, but the basic principles remain the same, even though
they may be executed in a different manner. For those not familiar
with the operations in a purchase ledger department, the paragraphs that follow help provide an overview.

Sorting the Post

Each day, any purchase invoices that arrive in the post need to be
checked against orders and delivery documents. It is usual to

check that the goods or services detailed on the invoice were received or executed satisfactorily before the invoice can be passed for payment. In a large organisation, where several departments may have individual responsibilities for purchases, copies of the invoices should be circulated to the individuals responsible for raising the order request, for an initial signature indicating that the invoice can be processed, or notifying any queries.

Once confirmed that the invoices are valid, they may be gathered together for input into the system. In some cases, purchase invoices may be entered in batches every week or so, rather than dealing with each day's input individually. This will largely depend upon the number of invoices being processed.

For any purchase accounts which are new — ie not already entered on the ledger — it is best to allocate account codes and other static details to the account ready for input by the operator. Keep all new accounts together at the top of the pile so that these can be processed first. The following information will *need* to be entered in respect of a purchase ledger account, so have this to hand before you begin, all other fields relating to purchase accounts are optional, and can therefore be entered at any convenient opportunity:

— the account number to be allocated to the supplier;

— the account name and address;

— the account analysis code;

— whether the account is open item or balance forward;

— the currency code, if the account is foreign.

If using the automatic payment processing facility, it may be worth entering the settlement discount and days-before-payment also, and this information can usually be derived from the invoice.

If entering several invoices in a batch, total all the invoices to be processed and make a note of this total (which should include VAT). You may wish to allocate your purchase analysis codes to the line items of invoices before they are entered to save time for the operator. Alternatively, a list of analysis codes should be provided so that they can be allocated quickly during the invoice processing procedure.

Account Name Update

If any new supplier accounts are to be added, set these up first. You cannot create a new supplier account at the time an invoice is posted. Check for changes of account details on existing supplier records, too. If changes have been made to the accounts, print a new list of suppliers to replace the old report.

Batch Check

If posting a batch of invoices, call up the creditors total screen from the processing menu and make a note of the amount displayed. Add to this total the total of all invoices and record the new figure. Keep this handy to check again after the invoices have been entered.

Senior Company Parameters

If foreign currency processing is used, make sure that the exchange rate table is kept up-to-date with the latest exchange rates for the day. You can, however, amend the rate at the time of posting an invoice.

Posting the Invoices

Enter each of the supplier invoices that have been approved for entry using the ledger processing function. Make sure that the VAT element of the invoice takes into account any settlement discount. In other words, the VAT will be the goods total, less settlement discount, multiplied by the VAT rate percentage.

Double check the analysis codes when breaking down the

invoice, and enter a suitable comment field to identify the nature of the goods or services being entered. Senior purchase ledger will automatically check for the existence of the destination nominal ledger account before allowing the analysis code to be accepted. In the case of incorrect analysis codes being used, which result in an invalid nominal account destination, corresponding values will be posted to the creditors suspense account.

Mark each invoice to indicate that it has been entered. This is usually done by assigning a file reference to the invoice. When all invoices have been entered, check the batch total by calling up the creditor total screen again. If the total displayed matches your batch total, you know that all invoices have been processed. When all are entered, print a list of invoices and credit notes.

Payment Processing

Payments can be processed in one of two ways: either manual postings for payments can be recorded in the ledger processing function, or the automatic payment procedure can be used. It is usual to ensure that invoices due for payment are passed by the appropriate authority (financial controller or buyer, for example) with a signature.

Whether using the automatic payment processing or not, print a suggested payments list, which details all those transactions due for payment and for which settlement discount applies. Use this as a guide to which invoices should be paid. Any invoices not passed for payment should be marked as being disputed. In Single-User purchase ledger, a special dispute and release transactions routine is provided for the purpose. In the case of Senior purchase ledger, the dispute flag can be assigned to transactions within the allocation procedure.

Another report that may be used to assess which accounts to pay is the aged creditors list. This will show you how much is outstanding aged across various accounting periods (usually monthly) up to three months and older. Obviously, one would normally clear the oldest debts first, unless an invoice is in dispute.

However, only the suggested payments routine will take into account disputed invoices and these are excluded from the report, and the aged creditors list will not identify transactions entitled to discount.

According to the suggested payments list, run the automatic payments routine with the appropriate pay date, or manually post the payments on the ledger. If using the cheque printing facilities, make sure that any manually posted payments have the reference 'CHQ'.

The cheques can then be printed, followed by a cheque listing. The authorised signatory must sign the cheques before they can be dispatched to the suppliers. If using the remittance advice facility, the automatic payment routine will print remittance advices at the same time, and these can be included with the cheque. Use the label printing function to label the envelopes for the payments, unless you are using window envelopes with the remittance advices.

Once all payments have been processed, print a list of payments and file with the audit trails for the purchase accounts. An account status report can be printed to show the latest account status of all suppliers (rather like the statement print function of the sales ledger).

Adjustments

If any adjustments need to be made to supplier accounts, carry these out before printing the list of payments and adjustments mentioned above.

Finally, take a backup copy of your purchase ledger data files at the end of the current processing.

Other Processing

Foreign currency account transactions will be subject to exchange discrepancies between the time the invoice is posted and the time a payment is made. Attention to fluctuating exchange rates and the frequent revaluation of outstanding creditor amounts will help you to time the payment of a transaction to your advantage.

The purchase ledger programs include a report for exchange discrepancies based on the foreign transactions, their original values and the revalued home currency equivalent. The report also shows the gain or loss on the transaction. Note that no actual discrepancy postings are carried out by this routine; it merely reports on the current value of the debt.

The transfer of purchase information to the nominal ledger can be carried out as often as required, but you should ensure that both this procedure and the printing of any user-definable analysis reports is carried out prior to the month-end. An audit trail is printed when information is transferred, and this is in fact the nominal journal for purchases (see also Chapter 6 for further details on integration and analysis).

Advance Postings

These operate like sales ledger advance postings and, indeed, probably have more significance in the purchase ledger. At the beginning of a new month, it is often the case that not all the previous month's invoices will have been received from suppliers. Some suppliers, for example, leave the dispatching of invoices until the end of the current month. Thus, invoices are received several days into the new month, which in fact relate to last month. Because of this, the period-end routine is generally delayed until such time as all invoices that are expected to be received have been posted. In the meantime, invoices may arrive for the new month, but if they are posted before last month's period-end routine is carried out, they will not be included in the new month's analysis reports.

To overcome this anomaly, Pegasus Senior purchase ledger provides an advance posting facility. This means that you do not have to wait until the period-end is performed for last month before entering transactions belonging to the current month. These transactions can be posted as 'advanced' (ie belonging to

the next period's analysis). When the period-end is finally executed, any advance posting transactions are retained for inclusion
in the new month's analysis file, and ignored in the previous
month's analysis file. An example of how this is effected using
dated transactions is shown in Chapter 4 on sales ledger.

PERIOD-END ROUTINE

Once all the processing has been done for the period, the month-
or period-end routine may be carried out. This checks that all
analysis items have been transferred to the nominal ledger, if the
option to integrate is set to Y, before proceeding. Similarly, if the
purchase ledger is integrated to job costing, the program checks
that all transfers have been made to the job records before the
period-end can continue.

Assuming that the above conditions are satisfied, the period-
end routine will offer the option of clearing the turnover figure recorded on all supplier accounts. If cleared each month, then the
turnover figure will always display the business carried out during
the month with any given supplier (based on invoices excluding
VAT). If left uncleared, the turnover accumulates throughout the
year. Flags on disputed invoices can also be cleared automatically,
though generally invoices in dispute remain so until such time as
authorisation is given to clear them. However, if the dispute flag
has been used simply to make the automatic payment routine
selective in the transactions processed (rather than for genuine
disputes or queries on goods supplied) this clearing option is quite
useful.

The routine itself will clear all open item account transactions
that have been allocated and, for balance forward accounts, produce a consolidated balance forward figure for previous period
transactions. Any accounts marked for deletion are removed, including those with zero balances if the appropriate parameter
option is set to Y. The purchase analysis file is cleared of all but
advance posting transactions, which themselves become current
transactions on the accounts. Accounts are reorganised into account number order.

6 Integration and Analysis

Integration of the sales, purchase and nominal ledgers and the analysis facilities are closely linked. While the analysis routines can be used simply as an independent reporting option to provide information about the goods that are sold and purchased, the codes involved in providing that report are also the key to the integration of the nominal ledger. This is because the two functions share the same file.

It is not apparent to new users of Pegasus (nor indeed to some experienced users) that the source of the information which forms the basis of sales and purchase integration to the nominal ledger, is in fact the analysis file and not the transaction file. One might be forgiven for assuming that the transactions which are transferred to the accounts within the nominal ledger should originate from a transaction file. However, invoices and credit notes for both sales and purchases are analysed during posting into one or more totals net of VAT. For example, an invoice received which contains both electrical items and office supplies might be split into two separate totals and analysed as two distinct types of expenditure.

This breaking down of a total invoice amount facilitates the analysis of the goods and services bought and sold so that, at any given time, one can ask 'how much did we spend on office supplies this month?' or 'how many size 8 black ladies' shoes did we sell this month?'. In order to answer questions such as these, a comprehensive method of analysing the invoices and credit notes is required, which is flexible enough to be used by any type of business. It is just as likely that another organisation might wish to find out 'how much business did we do on house contents insurance policies?' or 'what proportion of our sales were sold in the south east of England', or 'how much did we spend on training courses for our staff?'. All these are valid questions which are answered by properly analysing the content of invoices both sent to customers and received from suppliers. These transactions are the key to the answers — they provide the source of information.

Pegasus sales and purchase ledgers, like many other accounting system modules, are not intended to be used by any particular type of company, business, trade or industry sector. They are, as far as possible, general in the functions they provide, offering the accounting control required by all kinds of organisations that tend not to vary — an invoice is an invoice whatever the content. Yet, at the same time, the modules are flexible enough to allow certain functions to be used in such a way as to provide a degree of tailoring to the needs of the particular user. The questions posed above are quite diverse, yet the answers are all provided by the same analysis mechanism.

Such flexible analysis systems really have to be based on a coding system. This is because a code is ambiguous enough to be used to mean anything. A sales ledger analysis report which shows the following information:

    A123   1245.00
    A400   3864.00
    C091   2200.31
    S023   1108.24

can mean different things to different organisations. In a bookselling organisation, A123 might be a code which means fictional paperbacks, and the value shown alongside represents the value of sales of these items. To a firm of solicitors, A123 and its corresponding value might represent the income earned on writing wills. In other words, a code-based analysis means whatever is needed to the company concerned.

The same system of analysis applies to both sales and purchase ledgers alike. Both produce the analysis reports in precisely the same way. Each invoice or credit note posted has a corresponding analysis code for each element that a user requires to be analysed. Many invoices may be analysed to just one code, depending upon the content of the invoice, and others will require breaking down into sub-sections.

ABOUT ANALYSIS CODES

Analysis codes are themselves made up of more than one code. In the case of Single-User, there is an account-related analysis code, and the one related to invoice and credit note transactions. In the case of Senior, the same applies, except that the account code and stock reference (if integrated to stock control) are also used for analysis to the nominal ledger. Each part of the analysis coding facility is discussed step-by-step in the following paragraphs.

Account Analysis Code

The first part of a sales or purchase analysis code is the one stored in the account records. In Single-User, this is a two-character code; in Senior, a four-character code (see Figure 6.1 for an example).

Because this code is associated with an account record, it is generally used to identify the customer or supplier, the type of business they do, where they are, what they buy or sell, etc. All these examples relate to the account rather than individual items bought or sold. The code may be used to identify a representative who deals with the particular customer, for example. Hence a sales analysis can show what level of business has been achieved by individual sales personnel. Where foreign accounts are included in a ledger, the code may identify the country in which they operate, so that an analysis may be produced which shows what business has been undertaken with certain countries.

There are many possibilities, and the code will be used to suit various users according to the business which they are in. The difficulty comes in deciding how to use a code of limited size. One might consider that all of the above examples are useful forms of analysis, but the actual analysis reports that you produce will depend on how well you put the codes to use.

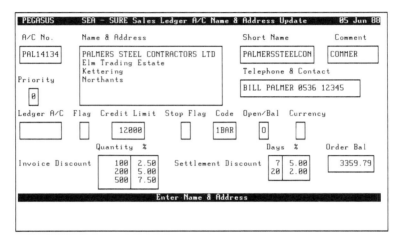

Figure 6.1   Account Record's Analysis Code

In the case of Single-User sales and purchase ledgers, the account analysis code is two characters long. The code will accept letters and numbers, so this means that you can use either one character for two different catergories of analysis, or two characters for one category.

— Two categories; each one character:

1st character up to 36 possible variations (A-Z, 0-9)
2nd character up to 36 possible variations (A-Z, 0-9)

An example of such a code might be:

● 1st character for customer type (R=Retail, W=Wholesale, M=Multiple, D=Distributor, I=Independent, P=Personal);

● 2nd character for county of operation (1=Cambridgeshire,

2=Norfolk, 3=Derby, 4=Hampshire, 5=Edinburgh, etc).

So that a code of R4 would identify a retailer in Hampshire.

In the case of purchase ledger, one character may be used for identifying the type of goods supplied.

— *One category; two characters available:*

In this case, there are 1,296 possible variations on the combinations of A-Z and 0-9. This alternative may be chosen if you only need to analyse the account under one category, and need more than 36 variations.

The Senior sales and purchase ledgers offer four characters for the analysis code, and therefore the possibilities are considerably extended:

— *One category; four characters:*
    1,679,616 variations

— *Two categories; each two characters:*
    1st two characters 1,296 variations
    2nd two characters 1,296 variations

— *Two categories; three characters and one character:*
    1st or last three characters 46,656 variations
    1st or last character remaining, 36 variations

— *Four categories; each one character:*
    1st character 36 variations
    2nd character 36 variations
    3rd character 36 variations
    4th character 36 variations

— *Three categories; two characters, one character and one character:*
    the two-character code, 1,296 variations
    each of the one-character codes, 36 variations

As an example, the following sales analysis code uses four categories of analysis for each sales account:

1st char	2nd char	3rd char	4th char
Country	*TypeArea*	*Sales rep*	
H = home	M = multiple	N = north	A
F = France	R = retail	S = south	B
B = Belgium	W = wholesale	E = east	C
S = Spain	I = independent	W = west	D

The code FMNA would therefore relate to a French multiple outlet sales account, in the northern area, attended by sales representative A. The code HREB would relate to a home retail account in the east, dealt with by representative B.

As you can see, the organisation of the account analysis codes is quite flexible, and particularly so with Senior sales or purchase ledgers. Each time an invoice or credit note is posted to a customer or supplier account, the analysis code associated with the account receiving the posting is *automatically* recorded with the value in the analysis file.

Invoice Analysis Code

The second part of the analysis code is the one entered when the goods value of an invoice or credit note posting is broken down at the time the transaction is posted (see Figure 6.2).

The codes entered at this stage are used to identify the content of the invoice or credit note in some way. For example, they may be used to describe a product group of items sold, such as men's shoes, nuts and bolts, consultancy services, accident insurance policies, etc. Like the account analysis code, the actual purpose of the code depends upon the type of analysis that the user wishes to obtain from the system, and how detailed the analysis is depends upon the way in which the code is utilised. The size of the analysis code is four characters for Single-User sales and purchase ledgers and eight characters for Senior ledgers. Characters may be either letters or numbers, and so for each individual character, up to 36 alternatives can be used, with considerable potential for the combination variations of the characters when grouped together.

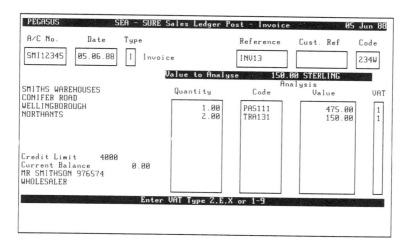

Figure 6.2 Invoice Posting Analysis

The following represents an example of a Senior purchase ledger invoice analysis code allocation of a shoe retailers:

1st char	2nd char		3rd char	4th char
Type	*Colour*		*Colour*	*Size*
L=ladies'	B	(blue)	L	0-9
M=men's	B	(black)	K	0-9
C=child's	B	(brown)	N	0-9

5th char	6th char	7th char	8th char
Size	*Style*	*not used*	*not used*
0-9	S=sandal		
0-9	B=brogue		
0-9	F=fashion		

In this example, the first character of the analysis code is used to represent the type of shoe purchased as being ladies', men's or child's. The next two characters are reserved for identifying the colour of the shoe — BL for blue, BK for black, BN for brown, etc. The following two characters are used to identify the size of the shoe — 05 (for size 5), 09 (for size 9), or in the case of continental sizes, 42, 43, 44, etc. Finally, the 6th character is used to identify the style of the shoe — B for brogue, S for sandal, F for fashion, etc.

Thus, a code of LBL06S would identify that the particular analysis line of the purchase invoice was for ladies', blue, size six sandals.

In this example, the analysis code provides a very specific breakdown of the line items of an invoice. However, the coding may be used for much broader descriptions. Indeed, if the analysis required is not at such a detailed level, it can be helpful to use as much of the code as possible to help identify the analysis item, so that reading the analysis report becomes much easier. For example, suppose an organisation was involved in selling photographic equipment, the invoice analysis codes used could be as follows:

         FILM   Films
         CAMS   Cameras
         LITE   Lighting
         DKRM   Darkroom supplies
         PROC   Processing
         CASE   Cases
         ACCE   Accessories

Each of the above is much more easily read in an analysis report than codes like LBL06S, which require much more familiarisation or constant reference to a list of code explanations. Using simple codes is best, provided the type of analysis required permits the use of enough characters to do so. You must remember that the one analysis code is used for all variations on the type of analysis report that you want. In the case of the shoes example, an analysis report could be printed of purchases by shoe style, purchases by size, purchases by type, etc, whereas the example for camera equipment is restricted to sales by product group only. There is no flexibility left in the photographic supplies example to analyse the type of cameras within the 'CAMS' category, and so on, unless you are also using Senior stock control, in which case the stock code can be used as part of the analysis coding, as described in your Senior sales ledger manual.

Whenever an invoice or credit note is posted on the sales or purchase ledgers, the goods value of the invoice is broken down into the various analysis line items, with up to ten entries allowed in any one posting (many more if using the invoicing module with sales ledger to post invoices). The analysis code associated with the analysis line is recorded with the appropriate value in the analysis file.

As mentioned previously, the account analysis code is also stored with the value automatically (ie it does not have to be entered, though Senior ledgers allow the amendment of the account analysis code for a specific posting). The two analysis codes are combined as one for each record in the analysis file. For example, suppose the following sales invoice was posted for photographic equipment, to a retail sales account which had an account analysis code of R1 (where R is for retailer and 1 is an area code):

Goods value of invoice: 457.75

Analysed to:

Code	Value
CAMS	325.75
FILM	15.50
DKRM	116.50

The total of the analysis values matches the goods value (ie the value before VAT is added) and so the transaction is stored in the files. In the analysis file, a record is stored for each analysis line of

the invoice, whereas only one record is added to the sales ledger
transaction file. The analysis file entry would include the following
information:

R1CAMS	325.75
R1FILM	15.50
R1DKRM	116.50

Notice that the account analysis code and the invoice analysis
codes are combined to form one analysis code entry with an
associated value. With this information stored in the analysis file,
a mechanism is required to extract information according to your
requirements. This is achieved through the entries in the ledger
parameter file and is explained in the following section.

DEFINING THE ANALYSIS

Continuing with the Single-User sales analysis example, each
character of the combined analysis code (of which there are six in
total) can be represented by a letter of the alphabet:

Character position:	1	2	3	4	5	6
Letter assigned:	A	B	C	D	E	F

The letters are the key to defining the type of analysis report
required. In the case of the current example, letters A and B (the
account analysis code) are used to represent the type of account
(retailer, wholesaler, etc), while letters CDEF are used to represent the characters of the product group invoiced (cameras, dark-
room equipment, films, etc).

Figure 6.3 shows the parameter input screen of Single-User
sales ledger, in which the analysis report definitions are entered.
Notice that for each analysis report option (of which there are
three), an entry is required for 'sequence' and another for 'description'. The critical entry is the sequence. This identifies what
you want an analysis of. Suppose an analysis of product group sales
over account type was wanted, the sequence entry would be as
follows:

CDEF/A

In this case, the letters CDEF indicate that the last four characters of the combined analysis code will be used in producing the report, and a further level of analysis will be provided of the account types defined by A.

```
 PEGASUS            SEA - SURE Sales Ledger Parameter Update      05 Jun 88
Settlement Discount - Days 1   : 7:  %  :  5.00:
Settlement Discount - Days 2   :30:  %  :  2.50:
VAT Code for Analysis          :LX7        :
VAT % For Option 10            :15.00:
Printer Type                   :1:
Analysis Code Minimum Size     :1:
                Maximum Size   :8:
Sales Analysis 1 - Sequence    :                    :
               - Narrative.    :                              :
Sales Analysis 2 - Sequence    :                    :
               - Narrative     :                              :
Sales Analysis 3 - Sequence    :                    :
               - Narrative     :                              :
Sales Analysis 4 - Sequence    :                    :
               - Narrative     :                              :
Sales Analysis 5 - Sequence    :                    :
               - Narrative     :                              :
Sales Analysis 6 - Sequence    :                    :
               - Narrative     :                              :
Report Ageing                  :   7:  14:28  :                :
              Enter Number of Days For 3rd Report Ageing
```

Figure 6.3   Example Sales Parameters

The oblique character separating the two helps the program to know where to divide the columns of the report and when subtotals should be printed. The general rule is that a sub-total is printed on every change of product group (ie the first category defined before the oblique). According to our invoice input then, the analysis report produced by such a sequence entry would include the following entry:

Group	Type	Value
CAMS	R	325.75
DKRM	R	116.50
FILM	R	15.50

The headings above the first two columns are actually the

'description' entries in the parameters, so in this case, they would be 'Group/ Type'.

Now let's see what happens when another invoice is posted, but this time to a wholesale account type which has an analysis code of W2 (wholesale, in area 2). Here are the invoice analysis entries:

Analysis Code	Value
CAMS	120.50
FILM	8.40

Now we re-run the analysis report which produces the following result:

Group	Type	Value
CAMS	R	325.75
	W	120.50
DKRM	R	116.50
FILM	R	15.50
	W	8.40

Notice that the new category has been included in the report for the wholesale invoice, but it only affects the two product group types which were included in the invoice.

From such a report, it is possible to determine such information as 'what value of cameras were sold to retailers compared to wholesalers?'.

If the second account analysis code character is used to determine the area in which a customer operates, this can be used to find answers to such questions as 'what values of each product group were sold in various areas of the country?'. Using the second character as part of the 'sequence' entry in the parameters, you would enter 'CDEF/B' as your selection with a description of 'Group/Area' in the parameters. The resulting analysis report would be something like this:

Group	Area	Value
CAMS	1	325.75
	2	120.50
DKRM	1	116.50
FILM	1	15.50
	2	8.40

Both the above examples show analysis reports based on two categories. It is just as simple to produce a report based on one category. 'What value of cameras was sold to all customer types in all areas?' would be answered with a parameter sequence entry of 'CDEF' only, and a description of 'Product Groups', producing the report:

Product Groups	Value
CAMS	446.25
DKRM	116.50
FILM	23.90

In this case, the totals of both example invoices have been added together under each group category.

These very basic uses of the analysis code already show how the careful assignment of analysis codes can ensure that a variety of analysis possibilities exist, using the same information in the one analysis file.

In Pegasus Senior, the analysis possibilities are extended further, for the simple reason that the analysis codes are longer, and therefore allow more categories to be defined. Furthermore, up to three levels can be included in one report, and the customer or supplier account code and the stock item reference (if stock control is used with the invoicing module) can be included as part of the analysis code.

Senior sales and purchase ledgers use the following letter assignments for the analysis codes:

A/c analysis code	*Invoice code*	*Account no*
ABCD	EFGHIJKL	MNOPQRST

Stock item and location code

UVWXYZ0123456789

The principle for assigning these letters to sequences in the parameters is the same as that described previously for Single-User. While it may look more complicated, the only difference is the size of the codes, and, therefore, the greater flexibility provided for analysis reporting.

For example, the fact that the account number itself can be included in the analysis facilities suggests that the careful assignment of account codes to customers or suppliers can itself provide a kind of analysis code. If the eight-character account code not only identifies a particular account, but also the area in which it operates, then this is one analysis category that does not need to be satisfied by the four-character account analysis itself, which means that the analysis code can be used for other categories.

WHY DOES THE ANALYSIS SEEM DIFFICULT?

The answer to this can be given in the form of an analogy. Getting to grips with the analysis facilities of Pegasus is rather like learning to drive; there are so many things to consider all at once when you begin — the clutch, the gears, looking in the mirror, road signs, the accelerator, steering, etc. If you are a driver, you will appreciate how, at first, the mastering of all these functions together seems so elusive, yet after practice, and in hindsight, it is difficult to comprehend what the difficulties were all about. A practised driver handles all the controls almost 'automatically'. This analogy represents the difficulties of learning the analysis facilities in the beginning. The many factors that have to be taken into consideration, including the different parts of the analysis code, seem daunting, but once mastered are really quite straightforward. The key, then, to understanding the analysis aspects of the ledgers is practice, and this is unfortunately not something that many users seem prepared to do. When you consider the speed with which the results can be obtained from the accounts once the mechanism of analysis is set up, one can hardly begrudge some investment of time in the first place.

The analysis facilities could be made easier to use, but this would result in restricted flexibility. Inevitably, the more flexible a system needs to be, the more investment in time and effort is required to set it up. As previously mentioned, Pegasus accounting software is not designed to be used by any particular type of business, and the analysis requirements will vary considerably. Giving guidance on the use of the facility inevitably requires using examples, and these examples may not be appropriate to the operation of your company. However, the principle has to be taught in one way or another. The examples also have to be simple and this tends to underplay the potential of the system.

In all, the best recommendation that can be given is to use the demonstration data files that are supplied with the software, and experiment. Do not concern yourself with how appropriate the examples are to your business; once you have learnt the procedures, you can soon apply them to any analysis requirement. Set up some accounts with analysis codes, writing down what each character of the analysis code stands for and do the same for a range of products or services. Half a dozen will do to start with — you do not need many to see the effect of obtaining different analysis reports from one set of invoice postings. Post half a dozen invoices onto the ledger (sales or purchase) using the analysis codes that you have defined.

Next, experiment with different sequence entries in the parameters, printing out an analysis report for each sequence you define. You can set up three at once in Single-User and six in Senior. This does not stop you changing the parameters as often as you like to try more examples, however. Look closely at the analysis reports to see how the sequence entries you make affect the content and breakdown of the report. The report options will ask if you want a list of all input and you should respond to this prompt by typing Y. This listing shows you all the analysis file entries that go to make up the analysis report (regardless of whether an analysis item is included in the final report or not). This will help you to understand what is being selected according to your sequence entries. The more examples you try, the more familiar you will become with what is happening, and this should set you up to sort out your own analysis requirements for the real accounting data.

One of the many considerations regarding the assigning of analysis codes which leads to further complications at the outset, is the fact that the same analysis codes are used to determine which accounts in the nominal ledger are to receive sales and purchase invoice and credit note values, and this is investigated in the following part of this chapter.

INTEGRATION

The sales and purchase ledgers integrate with the nominal ledger. This means that information about transactions, posted in either the sales or purchase ledgers, can be transferred to the nominal ledger without the need to re-enter any values. The sources of the information for the transfer are the respective analysis and transaction files of sales and purchase ledgers. In the analysis files are stored the values of invoices and credit notes posted to the ledgers, broken down into their various analysis codes. In the transaction file are the receipts, payments and adjustments that are posted to the accounts. The integration of receipts and payments is straightforward. Each receipt or payment is transferred to the nominal ledger with the following double-entry posting being made as a result:

In the case of sales receipts:

— debit the bank account;

— credit the debtors (sales) control account.

In the case of purchase payments:

— credit the bank account;

— debit the creditors (purchase) control account.

Receipts and payments may either be transferred individually (ie each transaction is recorded as a single entry in the bank account and control account) or as a batch posting. Generally, individual transactions are preferred, since this provides a means of reconciling the bank account with the statements received.

In the case of Senior, the bank account involved may optionally be selected at the time a posting is made. Otherwise, and in the case of Single-User, the bank account used is the one defined in the parameters of the nominal ledger.

Adjustment transfers are equally straightforward. All adjustments are posted to the suspense files of the sales or purchase ledgers, resulting in the following postings:

In the case of sales adjustments:

— credit the debtors suspense account;

— debit the debtors control account.

In the case of purchase adjustments:

— debit the creditors suspense account;

— credit the creditors control account.

Adjustments must be journalled out of the suspense account to the appropriate income or expenditure account to which they apply after the transfer has taken place. Receipts or payments and adjustments are transferred together, and a journal voucher is produced at the same time, taking the next available journal entry number from the nominal ledger files.

Invoices and credit notes use a different method of transfer, and because the differences between Single-User and Senior are significant enough they are discussed separately here.

Single-User Transfer

In the case of both sales and purchase ledgers, only the four-character invoice (credit note) analysis code is used for transfer, ie the two-character account analysis code is not involved in the transfer procedure, and is therefore only used for the analysis reports in sales or purchases.

The four characters within the code may each represent one or more corresponding characters of a nominal ledger account code (which is also four characters long) or none at all. For example:

Nominal accounts:
   SS01 — shoe sales account
   WS01 — wellington sales

Analysis codes from an invoice:
   SL09 — shoes, ladies', size 9
   WM11 — wellingtons, men's, size 11

The first character of the analysis code is the same as the first character of the nominal account code in each case. The last three characters of the sales invoice analysis codes vary according to the requirements of the sales analysis, and this does not have any influence on the nominal accounts. However, two accounts are kept in the nominal ledger: one to accumulate the value of all shoe sales, another to accumulate the value of all wellington boot sales.

The key to transferring the appropriate invoice values to the right nominal account is to use a 'mask'. This is a template which determines how much of the analysis code is used to specify the nominal account into which the values will be posted. This mask is stored in the nominal ledger parameter file and is four characters long. In the case of the above example, the mask entered would be as follows:

*S01

The first character of the mask is an asterisk. This acts as a 'gate' through which a character in the same position in the analysis code is 'let through' to the nominal ledger. The remaining three characters are predetermined and will always be S01 for all sales accounts in the nominal ledger. In other words, *all* nominal ledger accounts for sales end in the characters S01. The only character that changes is the first, and this identifies the product group (shoes, wellingtons, sportswear, or whatever).

When the integration routine takes place, and invoices are transferred to the nominal ledger, the analysis file is read by the nominal ledger programs and the template or mask is applied to each analysis code. The new code that results identifies the actual account number of the nominal into which the corresponding value will be posted — see Figure 6.4 below.

Invoice analysis code	S	L	0	9
Mask for sales	*	S	0	1
Nominal account number	S	S	0	1

Figure 6.4   Masking Facility

This shows how the nominal account code is made up of the first character of the invoice analysis code and the last three characters of the mask. The position of the asterisk determines which character is to be let through the mask. Any one or even all four of the mask characters can be an asterisk. So, if the mask was made up of four asterisks, the entire analysis code would be used to determine the destination nominal account. If no asterisks are used then all sales values, regardless of their analysis codes, would end up in the one nominal account for sales, as specified in the mask. The same procedure applies to purchase ledger, as this has its own mask in the nominal parameters.

You can see how the analysis code can influence the posting of invoice and credit note values to the nominal ledger, and this must be taken into consideration when allocating either analysis codes to invoice items, or nominal account codes, or both.

Remember that the key question which must be asked is what level of breakdown of sales and purchases do you need in the nominal ledger? For example, do you require separate sales accounts for itemising sales of different products or service types in the profit and loss account, or do you require separate purchase accounts for different types of purchases for budget control purposes?

If you answer your nominal ledger requirements first and then work backwards to your invoice and credit note analysis codes, you are more likely to produce a workable analysis and integration facility, and this is the reason why the nominal ledger is so often set up before the sales and purchase ledgers.

Senior Integration

Each sales or purchase invoice (or credit note) transaction includes the following codes for analysis and integration purposes, stored in the analysis file:

— the account analysis code (four characters);

— the item line (product) analysis code (eight characters);

— the currency code (one character from the account record).

The combination of a cost centre and nominal account code, that is to receive the posting of a corresponding value, can be made up from a selection of some, all, or even none, of the characters from the above codes.

Purchase ledger also provides information relating to the job number of cost codes if the purchase ledger is integrated to the job costing module. These will be ignored for the moment, since they are not necessary to describe the procedure of integration.

The parameters of the nominal ledger include a screen for defining a 'template', which is used to determine the nominal account and cost centre combinations to which values will be posted (see Figure 6.5 for an example).

```
 PEGASUS                    SEA - SURE Nominal Ledger              07 Oct 88

              Sales Ledger Nominal Code 8 Cost Centre Selection

Selection - Source    Name File  Analysis Code  Currency
          - Position  1 2 3 4    1 2 3 4 5 6 7 8     1
          - Code      A B C D    E F G H I J K L     $

Nominal Code Position  1 :P:S:  Predetermined Value - S
                       2 :S:C:  3rd Digit of Name File
                       3 :S:E:  1st Digit of Analysis Code
                       4 :P:X:  Predetermined Value - X
                       5 :P:0:  Predetermined Value - 0
                       6 :P:0:  Predetermined Value - 0
                       7 :P:0:  Predetermined Value - 0
                       8 :P:0:  Predetermined Value - 0

Cost Centre Position   1 :P:0:  Predetermined Value - 0
                       2 :S:F:  2nd Digit of Analysis Code
                       3 :P:0:  Predetermined Value - 0
                       4 :S:H:  4th Digit of Analysis Code
                    Press SPACE if O.K. - Else ESC if Not
```

Figure 6.5   Sales Codes in Nominal Parameters

Each character of a nominal account and cost centre code is represented by a number. For the account code it is from 1 to 8, and for the cost code from 1 to 4. For each of these character positions, it is possible to specify whether the character at that position will be preset according to a specific input in the parameters, or selected from one of the characters of the analysis codes displayed above. For example, suppose the account analysis code WN01 (representing a 'W'holesaler in the 'N'orth attended by sales representative '01') was used in the posting of a sales invoice. On the invoice, the following analysis entries would be made:

Code	Value	
CAM35PEN	2400.00	(35mm Pentax cameras)
CAM35NIK	1540.00	(35mm Nikon cameras)
ACCTRI01	76.50	(accessories, tripod model 01)

The analysis codes used here are for sales analysis purposes, so that reports can be produced on sales of various product ranges, manufacturers and product groups.

In the nominal ledger, the following accounts are set up:

Cost centre

WN00   Wholesale, northern area

Account

S0CAM000   Sales — cameras
S0ACC000   Sales — accessories

In the above example, an association can be seen between part of the analysis codes and the codes of the nominal ledger cost centre and account numbers. In other words, some of the characters are predetermined and others may be selected from the analysis codes. The following entry in the nominal ledger parameters would ensure that the appropriate integration took place:

Nominal code position

1   Predetermined — S (for sales)
2   Predetermined — 0 (not used)
3   Selected from 1st digit of analysis code
4   Selected from 2nd digit of analysis code
5   Selected from 3rd digit of analysis code
6   Predetermined — 0 (not used)
7   Predetermined — 0 (not used)
8   Predetermined — 0 (not used)

Cost centre position

1   Selected from 1st digit of account analysis code
2   Selected from 2nd digit of account analysis code
3   Predetermined — 0 (not used)
4   Predetermined — 0 (not used)

Those characters that have been predetermined indicate what *all* sales accounts will contain as standard:

Cost centre   Account code

00   S0*000

Where the asterisks are shown, one can regard these as 'gates' through which selected characters from the various analysis codes are permitted to be 'let through', thus completing the destination nominal ledger codes into which the corresponding values will be posted. In this example, the following postings would be made:

Cost centre	Account code		Dr	Cr
WN00	S0CAM000	Sales — cameras		3940.00
WN00	S0ACC000	Sales — accessories		76.50
	Debtors control account		4016.50	

The debtors control account will be the one specified in the nominal parameters, and analysis codes will not play a part in the entry in this account. It will always reflect the double-entry posting of the aggregate of all sales account postings.

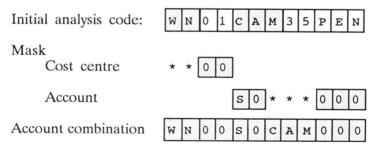

Figure 6.6   Combining Analysis and Preset Codes

The principles described here apply as much to purchase ledger as they do sales ledger. In each case the characters that make up the nominal codes may include specific selections from the analysis codes, together with predetermined characters, and the positions do not have to match as they do in the Single-User mask facility, but can be displaced to a different character position (see Figure 6.6 for an example).

GENERATION NUMBERS

Each of the three ledger parameter data files contains a special reference called a generation number. This number identifies the current number of transfers between modules that have taken place. The sales and purchase ledgers each have their own generation number and the nominal ledger has two. Whenever a transfer of information from sales to nominal or purchase to nominal takes place, all relevant generation numbers are updated. When you begin to use the modules for the first time, the status of the generation numbers is as follows:

Sales ledger parameters:

    Generation number   1

Purchase ledger parameters:

    Generation number   1

Nominal ledger parameters:

    Sales generation number   1

    Purchase generation number   1

As soon as a transfer is carried out (for example, sales ledger invoices and credit notes) from one ledger to nominal, these generation numbers will be affected according to the ledger involved in the transfer. In the case of a sales transfer then, the sales ledger's generation number is incremented by a value of 1, as is the nominal ledger's generation number for sales.

This results in the following change of generation numbers in the parameter files:

Sales ledger parameters:

    Generation number   2

Purchase ledger parameters:

    Generation number   1

Nominal ledger parameters:

    Sales generation number   2

    Purchase generation number   1

Each time transfers are carried out, the generation numbers are incremented. If the transfer involves sales ledger, then the two sales ledger generation numbers are updated, and likewise for purchase transfers, the purchase generation numbers are updated.

The reason for keeping these numbers maintained is to ensure that the ledgers keep in step with one another. Suppose a backup of the data files is taken with the generation numbers shown in the previous example. Following this, another transfer of sales is carried out which increments the generation numbers in the sales ledger parameters and nominal parameters for sales to 3. At this point, an unfortunate occurrence takes places which affects the data files (such as a power failure), which makes the sales ledger data files unreadable. Reverting to the backup that was taken before, the user restores the sales ledger data only. But this set of data included a parameter file which indicated that the current generation number was 2. The result can be shown by the following example:

	Sales params	*Nominal params (sales)*
Generation numbers when backups were taken	2	2
Generation numbers after a further update	3	3

| Generation numbers at the time of data corruption | 3 | 3 |
| Generation numbers after restoring sales data only | 2 | 3 |

This example clearly shows that as a result of restoring only the sales ledger data files, there is now a mismatch between the sales ledger's generation number and the one that the nominal ledger believes to be the most recent for sales. If the operator were to attempt a transfer of sales to nominal at this stage, the program would inform of a generation number mismatch, and prevent the transfer from going ahead, since if it did there would be a strong possibility that the nominal ledger accounts would contain the same sales information twice.

Another circumstance in which a mismatch can occur is when data files are permanently stored on floppy disks, as opposed to a hard disk (generally only applicable, therefore, to Pegasus Single-User). Disks can get mixed up, and if they are not properly labelled, it is possible that a disk used for a previous transfer could be inserted into the disk drives ready for transfer to the current nominal ledger. The generation number checking ensures that only those sets of data that are in step are used for updating, and not an older disk, which has already transferred information to the nominal ledger.

Pegasus programs provide a parameter option that allows the generation number checking to be ignored and there is really only one reason why this should be done. Occasionally, users may want to keep separate sets of data files for sales ledger processing, but transfer all data to the one nominal ledger. Clearly, it is not possible for a single nominal ledger to be in step with more than one sales ledger, and a generation mismatch would occur the moment a transfer was attempted from a different set of data files. This parameter option, which allows generation numbers to be ignored, enables users operating in this way to update different data sets as required. The disadvantage is that the user loses all security against a mistake involving the incorrect disks being made.

As a word of warning, the parameter option should never be used to remove a valid generation number mismatch problem. Misuse of the option in this way will almost certainly result in the nominal ledger containing duplicated sales or purchase values.

7 Report Generator

One of the most useful features of the Pegasus ledgers is the report generator function provided with each module. It is a facility that allows information already stored in the data files of the ledgers to be extracted and organised to produce a report or file output of your choice. The report generator option is provided on the main menu of the sales, purchase and nominal ledgers, for both Single-User and Senior. For both suites of programs, the operation of the report generator is almost identical. The only variation of any significance is the data that can be selected.

The data files of each module may be accessed independently, but there is no facility to combine the data in the files of sales ledger with those of nominal ledger, for example. The report generator accesses only the data files of the module from which it is selected. However, this is not a major restriction, since most reports are based on only one module at a time and further integration of information has to be carried out with other software.

SELECTING THE REPORT CONTENT

For sales and purchase ledgers, the following data files may be accessed to extract information in particular combinations for reporting purposes:

— the names file;

— the transaction file;

— the analysis file.

In addition to these data files, another set of information fields may be called upon and these are items that are 'calculated' by the programs, rather than being stored in a particular file.

The nominal ledger report generator provides access to the following data files:

— the names file;

— the transaction file;

and a calculated set of information fields. Figure 7.1 shows an example selection screen for sales ledger.

```
 PEGASUS              SEA - SURE Sales Ledger              21 Jun 88
 Account No.  Disc.1 Amt.  Account No.  Currency     Type I or C  Unallocated
 A/C Name     Disc.1 %     Tran Date 1  Home Balnce  Analysis Cd  Current
 Address L1   Disc.2 Amt.  Tran Date 2  Exchge Rate  VAT Code     1 Month Old
 Address L2   Disc.2 %     Age in Days  Home Value   Value        2 MonthsOld
 Address L3   Disc.3 Amt.  Trans Type   Delivry A/C  Quantity     3 MonthsOld
 Address L4   Disc.3 %     Reference                 Account No.  4 MonthsOld
 Address L5   Last Pay.    Total Value               Anal Date 1  5+MonthsOld
 Tele & Cont  Last Act.    VAT Value                 Anal Date 2
 A/C Code     Ledger A/C   Balance                   Reference
 A/C Type     Address Flg  Paid Ind.                 Advance Ind
 Cr. Limit    Order Bal.   Month Alloc               Prof Margin
 Turnover     Currency     Day Created               Stock Ref
 Last Inv.    Del.Addr.Ct  Cust. Ref.                Foreign Val
 Current Bal  Short Name   Set.Disc. 1               Foreign Flg
 Comment      Stop Flag    Set.Days 1
 Set.Disc. 1  Priority     Set.Disc. 2
 Set.Days 1                Set.Days 2
 Set.Disc. 2               Advance Ind
 Set.Days 2                Advance Val
        Cursor Key Through Screen. Press SPACE at Required Fields
```

Figure 7.1   Sales Ledger Selection Screen

The columns of the selection screen each represent the various data files. For example, the first column of the screen in Figure 7.1 shows the fields stored within the sales ledger names file, ie the file which stores the names and addresses of the customer account records. Notice that there is information in this file not normally displayed when a customer account is called onto the screen. The account balance, for example, is not seen in the name and address update routine, but the value is recorded in the names file, and is referred to whenever an account enquiry is requested. Since the field resides in the names file, it is made available to the report generator programs.

The next column relates to the transaction file, and each of the fields stored within this file is presented on the selection screen. The third column contains the analysis file entries, and then the last column shows what calculated fields are also available.

The principle behind the report generator is that items from the selection screens are selected for inclusion in a report. Each selection represents a 'column' on a report, as shown in Figure 7.2.

```
Fields selected:     Account Number
                     Account Name
                     Turnover
                     A/c Balance


A/C No.    Account Name                                    Turnover       A/c Balance

XXXXXX    XXXXXXXXXXXXXXXXXXXXXXXXXXXXXXXX 99999999.99   99999999.99
```

Figure 7.2   Field Selections

This shows the 'default' layout of fields selected in the order shown. The actual order is defined by use of a letter from A to O, such that the first column on the left will be field A, the next column field B, the next column field C, and so on.

This selection process also has to take into account columns that are not based on the selection of a field from the lists given, but ones that you might want to include based on a calculation performed on other fields selected. For example, suppose you wanted a report which showed turnover as a percentage of the total annual sales of the company. This column of the report cannot be extracted by simply selecting a field, since there is no field stored which represents this requirement. The column has to be arrived at by calculation. This means that the column must be provided for within the report layout, and must have a letter of its own to determine the placing of the column in the report corresponding to those already defined. For example:

Order criteria: A   Account number
                   B   Account name
                   C   Turnover
                   D   Turnover as a percentage of total sales
                   E   Account balance

Item D is provided for by omitting this character when defining the other fields that are selected from the lists.

Since the new column is going to be numeric, the system will set its length to the maximum length for number fields (11 in the case of Single-User, 13 in the case of Senior). The lengths of all fields default to their maximum field length. The account name, for example, will default to 30 characters, the account number to four (if Single-User) or eight (if Senior). However, the report generator allows these lengths to be reduced or extended.

The effect of reducing the field length is to cut off the field when it is printed, and this is generally done when many items need to be fitted onto a finite paper width, and the full length of the field is not necessary for the purposes of the report. For example, half the account name field might be sufficient to identify the account, and save 15 characters of width; sufficient to include another numeric column.

The effect of extending the field length is to open up space between columns. Unless otherwise amended, each column of a report is separated by two character spaces. If more space is required between one column and another, this has to be provided by extending the field length of a selected column. For example, if the account number field of eight characters is left unchanged, the account name field (using the above example) will start printing at column ten (two spaces after the end of the account number). If, however, the account number field is extended to 12 characters, then four more spaces are added to the two already provided, thus the account name column begins printing at position 14 from the far left.

Spacing the report is particularly important when there are many columns to include, and it is sometimes helpful to plan the layout on paper first, perhaps using graph paper or a grid to represent one character space for every one available on the width of your computer stationery. Your printer is normally likely to accept 80 or 132 column width stationery (unless you are using a laser printer) so this fact must be accommodated in your report design considerations.

Another way of affecting the field length is to set it to zero. This means that the field selected will not be printed on the report at all. The reason for doing this is that some fields may need to be selected only for inclusion in a calculation, ie they are not to be included as a column in the report, but need to be selected anyway so the value of the field can be used in calculating another column.

CALCULATED ITEMS

To specify calculations, fields need to be referenced according to their corresponding letters. Arithmetical symbols can be included as well as constant values. Using the previous example, the calculation of turnover as a percentage of total sales would be specified as follows:

C/105,985*100

where 105,985 is a constant value representing the total annual sales (which must be provided as a constant input, since it cannot be selected from the fields available). The above calculation offers the content of column D, which, being numeric, will take the default field size of 11 or 13 characters.

Using calculated fields is what makes report generator the powerful facility that it is. Without the inclusion of calculations, the report generator provides only another way of printing the same kind of information included in standard reports, though you can be more selective about what is included and the order in which items appear. Fields referred to in calculations must be those that have been selected prior to the calculation column.

If the following selections were made:

A   1st field (column)
B   2nd field (column)
C   3rd field (column)
D   calculated column
E   4th field (column)
F   5th field (column)

then item D, the calculated item, can only be based on the content of columns A, B and C, and not E and F. In other words, a formula such as $B-C$ or $A+B+C$ is acceptable, but a formula such as $C*E$ or $B+F$ would not work, since at the time the D column is being printed, the information in columns E and F is not available for the calculation. Calculated items can themselves be included in other calculated fields so long as they are specified in the right order.

SELECTION CRITERIA

For any selected and calculated item, selection criteria can be assigned to determine what is included in a report. Selection criteria are instructions that tell the program what is acceptable for inclusion in a report. Assume that the names file of a sales ledger contained the following account codes:

A001   B003   D001
A002   C001   D002
B001   C002   D003

If the account code field is selected for the report generator design and the following selection criteria are applied:

ne A??? and ne D???

the result will be that only the following codes are selected:

B001 B003 C001 C002

In other words, the selection criteria excluded all codes beginning with A or D. The various selection criteria that can be used include those that choose fields equal to something, not equal to something, less than a specified number or more than a specified number, and these criteria can be linked together to define precisely what should be selected.

The programs, and the manuals that accompany them, refer to operators, literals and logical operators. Operators refers to the operation that is carried out in the selection criterion. For example, the operator 'eq' carries out the 'select if the record is equal to...' operation. Literals are the 'somethings' that selection criteria act on.

When one enters a criterion like 'eq ABC', it is the 'ABC' that is the literal — it 'literally' describes a field or part of a field. A logical operator is an 'AND' or an 'OR'. It is used to link two or more selection criteria together so that more specific instructions about what is included can be specified. For example, 'eq A001 AND eq B001' would select both literals 'A001' and 'B001'.

SORTING

So far, the selection of items to be included in the report has been discussed. Once these items have been selected, they can be sorted into a particular order. Sorting is defined by choosing an item on which to sort — any field can be used for sorting, including calculated fields — and then specifying whether the sorting is to be in ascending or descending order. Some people get confused about the two types of sorting, so here are some examples to illustrate them. Basically, ascending means that the values ascend from the lowest value to the highest and descending means that values descend from the highest to the lowest:

Ascending order examples		*Descending order examples*	
2,000	A001	10,000	I001
3,000	B001	9,000	H001
4,000	C001	8,000	G001
5,000	D001	7,000	F001
6,000	E001	6,000	E001
7,000	F001	5,000	D001
8,000	G001	4,000	C001
9,000	H001	3,000	B001
10,000	I001	2,000	A001

THE FILES INVOLVED

Report generator is sub-divided into four programs relating to the following functions:

— the report design process;

— the data selection process;

— the sorting procedure;

— the printing routine.

Each of these processes can be carried out independently, though the first time a new report is designed, the program gives you the option of moving straight onto the next routine. The sorting procedure is only run if sorting is specified, otherwise it is skipped.

When a new report is designed, the design format is stored in the following data file:

<filename>.REP

where <filename> includes the name of the report design. These are preceded by a character which identifies the module to which the design belongs: S for sales, P for purchase and N for nominal ledger. The file extension .REP indicates that the file contains a report design.

When the data for the report is selected, it is extracted from the various data files of the module, according to the selection criteria defined in the design. This data is stored in a file as follows:

<filename>.SEL

The filename will be the same as the corresponding report design, but the file extension .SEL indicates that the file contains selected data for the report.

A control file is also stored on the disk, and is used for information about sorting and for other data in relation to the report generator. This takes the format:

<filename>.CTL

There is no 'printing' file unless the report is spooled, in which case, the normal .SPL file extension is used.

When a report has been printed, the program offers the chance to remove the data files connected with the report. If the operator responds by typing Y, the .SEL and .CTL files are deleted, but the design remains intact in the .REP file, so that different data can be selected from the files based on the same design. This is useful if the report is to be produced on a period basis, and each period provides new data to select from.

If the data files are kept, then the same set of selected data can be used to reprint the report further (rather like a spool file), once sorting has taken place. This means that the same set of data can be resorted into a different order if the report design is changed. This may be an advantage in cases where a great deal of data is selected, and the selection procedure takes some time. The sorting routine is always much faster than the selection process, which has to search through every record in the data files to see if it matches the selection criteria.

Report generator also outputs other files and these are described next.

SPECIAL FILE OUTPUT

If the information selected through the report generator can be
used in other software packages, the printing routine can be used
to output the content in a variety of file formats:

— Multiplan file (.MPL);

— Lotus 1-2-3 file (.WKS);

— IBM Planning Assistant file (.IPA);

— Comma separated variables file format (.CSV).

The first three of these are spreadsheet file formats for well
known spreadsheet software packages. The fourth format is one
that can be used by many application software packages such as
databases, word processors, other spreadsheets, integrated packages, etc.

Using these file output options, report generator not only
becomes a means of extending the reporting capabilities of the
standard modules, but provides the mechanism for exporting
information from the accounts into other applications, where they
may be manipulated further or used for new reports and processing requirements beyond those given in the accounting system. A
word processor or database that can read the .CSV file format for
producing mail shots to selected sales ledger accounts is one example. Another example is the output of nominal accounts information for depreciation accounting, budget analysis and cash flow
forecasting.

You will need to refer to the appropriate documentation associated with the software packages with which you choose to link
the files, to see how the file formats can be used for linking
externally produced information. To clarify comma separated

variable files, however, these are files in which each data element (field) included in the file is separated from the next by a comma: field 1,field 2,field 3,field 4, etc. This information enables another software package to read the content of the file on the basis that when a comma is reached, that is the end of the current variable, and the next one can be read. Also, text fields are identified by being enclosed in quotes: "text field", whereas numbers are not: 99999.99. This helps a program distinguish between the two field types.

USING REPORT GENERATOR TO ADVANTAGE

Report generator is often overlooked by Pegasus users. This is perhaps because the standard reports provided within the module's menus are quite comprehensive, and, not surprisingly, cover the most important requirements for sales, purchase and nominal ledger accounting. Also, the report generator function requires a little more time and effort than other processes within the system, a resource which is scarce in many cases.

However, there is a great deal that can be obtained from the report generator, if a little imagination is applied to the reporting possibilities of the data which already lies in the data files, waiting to be extracted for management and accounting control assistance.

It is sensible to make the data that is stored work for you as hard as it can, and to your advantage. A couple of ideas have been discussed in this book already. One, for example, was the use of the report generator to extract information from the sales ledger accounts about their period turnovers. This information could be used to calculate commission for sales representatives. Suppose the following fields were selected:

A   Account number
B   Account name
C   Turnover

Using a calculated column D with the following formula:

C*.15

where 0.15 is the percentage commission due on the turnover with each customer for that month. The new calculated column included on the report can then show, either for each account or for each sales representative, how much commission is due, according to the selection criteria. A representative may be defined by a character in any of the account record fields, such as the analysis code.

This example points to a particular aspect of report generator which is quite valuable. The selection criteria can be quite specific about what is selected, and even part of a field can be used to select records for inclusion in a report. This means that imaginative use of the fields in records, whether they are account records or transaction records, can produce an extensive variety of report possibilities. In the last chapter, the use of the analysis codes was discussed, with emphasis on how the need to consider both the analysis and integration requirements at the same time can mean some careful planning is required. With the report generator, however, any analysis requirement missing or omitted from the standard sales or purchase analysis facilities can be incorporated by the use of other fields within the system.

For example, part of the nominal account description field can be utilised for special analysis of certain groups of accounts. In the chapter on nominal ledger it was mentioned that it is not often that the chart of accounts, when first set up, remains suitable for all reporting and integration requirements later on. Most new users of the system find that, after using it for a period of time, the structure of the accounts may need changing, and the reason for this is often related to the use of account numbers. Yet, account numbers cannot be changed for existing records, which means that all the accounts and balances would need to be re-entered from scratch. The alternative is to think about ways of using other fields within the records, like the description, to enter special codes for grouping and selection of records for certain reports with the aid of the report generator. In this way, no change need be made to the original structure of the accounts.

In the case of sales and purchase ledgers there are fields, such as the comment field, which may be used as another analysis field. With up to 15 characters available, that would considerably enhance the standard analysis facilities. The address fields can be used also. For example, the chapter on analysis shows that part of the account analysis code might be used to identify the area in which the account operates, yet the address could be used for this purpose.

The main thing to consider is that if you wish to use an address field to record an area, such as a county, then the name of the county must appear in the same place for each account, otherwise the report generator selection criteria will not work. Perhaps you would need to lay down a rule that the fourth address line for all account records is used only for the name of the county, regardless of the length of the rest of the address. If such a rule was not adhered to, then short addresses might find the county entered in the third field, while long addresses would have it in the fourth field. Similarly, the post code may be used for area sorting and selecting. Continuing with this example, if the fourth field of the address was the county, the following selection criterion could be entered to report on all accounts operating in the West Midlands area:

eq West Midlands

As a special point, you should realise that in this case, any account with the county entered as WEST MIDLANDS would be ignored. This is because the county name is entered in upper case and the selection criteria has been entered in a mix of upper and lower case characters. Particular care should be exercised in fields that allow upper and lower case characters, and perhaps a general rule of field entry for operators should be defined for those fields that are likely to be required for selection and sorting purposes. In the case of sorting, upper case characters are always sorted 'before' lower case characters, or to put it another way, in an ascending order sort, upper case characters would appear first.

Another example of a report not provided as standard in the

Pegasus sales ledger is one showing the number of days outstanding on transactions for particular customers. This statistical information can be used to help cashflow forecasts or to simply gauge the speed with which a particular customer is likely to pay, which can be used to assign order processing priorities. To produce a report such as this, the average age of debts needs to be assessed, and this means the report will need to be completed in two stages.

The first stage involves selecting all outstanding invoice transactions. The fields required might include the following selections from the transaction file:

— account number;

— age in days;

— transaction type (selection criterion 'eq INV');

— paid indicator (selection criterion 'eq !').

The paid indicator is used to select transactions that remain unallocated (and therefore outstanding). The transaction type selects all invoice amounts only. The length of both of these fields should be set to 0, since they are not required in the report output, but simply used as selection criteria.

When defining the report details, the age-in-days column should be marked for totalling and then the total breaks option should be set for a change of account number. Having entered suitable headings, the printed report will take the following format:

Account	Age (days)	
XXXXXXXX	999	(one line per transaction)
	999	(sub-totals)

The information on this report shows the number of days

outstanding for each selected transaction, separated into accounts. The average for any given account could be calculated by
dividing the sub-total by the number of transaction lines on the
account. Stage two of the report involves finding the total average
age of debt.

During the report selection procedure, the screen displays the
number of records selected according to the criteria. At the end of
the selection, the number displayed represents the total of all
outstanding transactions included in the report. Make a note of
this number. When the report has been printed, the last total
should reflect the total number of days outstanding for all transactions on all accounts. By dividing this number by the total number
of transactions selected by the procedure, you have the average
length of debt, in days, for the sales ledger. This value can be used
to assess cash income projections in a cash flow budget. In other
words, if you have a lot of slow paying customers on your accounts,
this will be reflected by the average number of days. If your terms
are 30 days, and your average is 45, you know that on average
payments take at least two weeks after the due date before they
are settled. Note that this is not a measure of the actual time
between invoice date and payment date, only the age of debts, but
the information can help you assess the state of your ledger in a
different way to the aged debtors report, which is based on values
due for specific periods, rather than an actual number of days.

Examples for the use of report generator are numerous and
clearly they cannot all be dealt with here. In any case, it is the
nature of a company's business that dictates what sort of management information should be provided for better business controls.
The most important thing to grasp about the facility is that it has
considerable potential, and the more thought put towards what
use can be made of the information, the more uses one will find.
The previous example serves only to illustrate the way in which
one should think about the potential of the facility. Try looking at
the reports that you get as standard menu options and ask yourself
the question 'is there another way in which this information could
be printed, so that it is more useful?'. Perhaps simply the order in
which information appears could be changed.

A simple turnover report sorted in order of ascending turnover value is one of the simplest reports that could be produced, yet it immediately gives you a 'top twenty' chart of your best customers. A similar report for the purchase ledger could feed information to a buyer about the amount of business done with particular suppliers; information which could be used to secure better purchasing deals. Another simple report is one which shows the credit limit and turnover fields together for all accounts. This can be used to assess whether credit limits should be extended or not.

The use of the selection criteria alone can improve the usefulness of reports. Within nominal ledger, it may be used to print budget reports selected by cost centres, which simply show the information pertaining to individual departments. The printed copies can then be circulated among the department heads as the basis for a management discussion on budgetary control.

Using calculated columns provides considerably more potential. Even calculating the difference between the account balance and the calculated fields for debts older than 90 days (three months), provides an extended aged debtors report that shows those 4 and 5 months old.

Total breaks provide ways of obtaining sub-totals not normally available with the standard reports of the ledgers. Nominal ledger is perhaps the exception, with sub-totalling available as an option on the trial balance for example, but there are applications for printing sub-totals on changes of other fields besides the account code, and this can only be achieved with the report generator. Used with the 'page throw' facilities, sub-divisions of a report can be separated on the listing paper for circulating to various individuals.

Turnover and outstanding debt information grouped by sales representative's operating area could be handed out to the sales force for information about the status of their account customers, for example. Printing a list of accounts on stop, separated by sales department, for order processing control is another simple but effective report possibility.

The usefulness of report generator is down to how much one is prepared to do to maximise on the efficiency of the information stored in the data files. The more the facility is used, the more applications one tends to think of.

8 How to Get More

Given that, like many accounting software packages, the Pegasus ledgers are standard systems for general use, the likelihood that the functions provided will exactly match the requirements of an individual company are fairly remote. Somewhere along the way, most organisations have to compromise with the facilities of an accounting system unless they are prepared to pay large sums of money to have a system designed and programmed exclusively for their own use. However, the trend has been for most companies to use standard packaged software and, in response to this, software houses such as Pegasus endeavour to build in flexibility in the software. With the Pegasus ledgers, this flexibility comes in the form of parameters — options that control the way certain functions of the software perform. To use a particular function in a certain way, the parameter option is set accordingly. Foreign currency accounting is a good example. In Pegasus Senior, a parameter option controls whether this facility is used or not. By omitting the option, the fields and prompts relating to foreign currency processing are left out from the screens, so as not to hinder the operation of the software for those who do not require the function. Only a report option remains, which can easily be ignored.

Another form of the flexibility that has already been discussed is the analysis of sales and purchase ledgers. By using a coding system, the analysis suits requirements from service industries to mail order companies. Inevitably, the more facilities included in a software package, the more complicated it is going to be to operate, and the more likely it is that a large section of the program will be redundant to an individual organisation. This latter problem is exacerbated by the fact that the more comprehensive the facilities in the software, the more expensive it will be, and no one would be pleased about paying for features that are not appropriate for their own needs.

So how do you get more from your system, so that it can be operated more closely to your requirements, without making the existing software redundant or over-complicated? There are a number of options and these are discussed in the following paragraphs.

VERTICAL MARKET SOLUTIONS

A term used in the computer industry for describing software packages that are designed for specific sectors of industry and commerce is 'vertical market'. Vertical market software packages, therefore, provide functions that are suited to particular types of business operation, such as a baker's package, a hotel booking system, a double-glazing window assembly system, etc. Each of these software packages is aimed exclusively at those organisations who need processing requirements that are not catered for in standard, horizontal market applications.

One area of business software which is subject to considerable variation within the software packages is invoicing procedures. The requirements for invoicing the square metreage of carpets is quite different from those of an advertising agency. The needs are probably so diverse that no one computerised invoicing system can necessarily do both jobs well (depending upon how much automation of calculations is required). To satisfy these needs, many software authors write packages that will be suitable for the processing requirements of these vertical markets and integrate these with standard accounting ledgers. The ledgers do not need to change so much from one type of business to another — the need to store information about who your customers are, how much they owe and what transactions are outstanding probably does mean the same thing to an advertising agency and a carpet wholesaler. So the ledgers tend to be the backbone of an accounting system. Extending the capabilities, therefore, means looking for systems that are separate from the main accounting system.

Not all systems will integrate to any accounting system of course. The file formats that store the data contained in the Pegasus ledgers are peculiar to Pegasus, and are not the same as those used by other accounting software authors. Hence, any vertical market software package that is to be used with the Pegasus ledgers, must be able to recognise the file formats of Pegasus and read and write information back and forth between its own files and those of Pegasus.

There are a considerable number of such applications on the market. This is probably due to the long history in the microcomputer industry afforded by Pegasus Software Limited and the large user base that has subsequently arisen. The larger the number of users for a standard accounting package, the more profitable it is for an independent software house to write and sell tailor-made or vertical market packaged software that integrates with that system. This has certainly been the case for Pegasus Software Limited.

There are software packages for almost every conceivable industry sector from hire companies to turf accountants, with a whole range of add-on utility programs for discount matrix requirements, file manipulation, housekeeping functions and the like.

Finding out about such systems can be achieved in two ways: either by contacting your Pegasus dealer, who can either directly or indirectly (via Pegasus Software Limited) advise on the available vertical market software packages that integrate to the Pegasus system, or by looking for the software packages that perform the required functions and checking whether they integrate to Pegasus. The sources of information about such systems can be either software catalogues or other dealers. Many of the add-on software systems available are written by programmers employed in software dealerships, and any Pegasus dealer should be able to provide information.

DATABASES

Another way of extending the system is by using database applications and application generators. These are software packages that can be used to design and run an application which may have any kind of use, depending upon how it is structured. It is a kind of simple-to-use programming facility that enables special data processing requirements to be handled without the software having been specifically written for the job. Instead, the user of the database designs his or her own application software. Some accounting systems are developed using application generators, for example, rather than, as in the case of Pegasus, being written in true programming code.

If your organisation has a special data processing requirement that cannot be satisfied by the standard accounting system, the solution can probably be provided by the use of a database. Coupled to this is the fact that the report generator provides a means of selecting information from the accounting system and outputting this in a file format that can be read by most database applications (the comma separated variables format), which means that your tailored application can make use of data already stored in the accounting system's files (see Figure 8.1).

The disadvantage of database and application generator software systems is that they are, on the whole, quite complicated systems, which require a great deal of investment in time and effort before they can be of benefit. If you have no technical expertise, many systems (though not all) can be too complicated to attempt to use without considerable guidance.

There is a lot to learn about using a software package as flexible as a database, compared to using the predefined functions of an accounting system. As a way round this, you may find that your dealer can set up the application you require for you using a database or application generator, including the report generator links necessary to produce a well integrated system. You will, of course, have to pay for the development time and knowledge offered by the dealer in these circumstances.

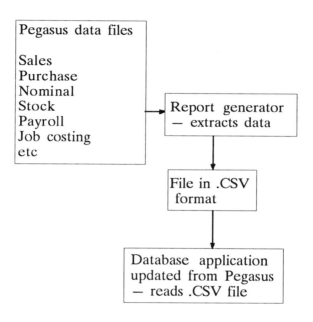

Figure 8.1   Database Integration

PEGASUS INTEGRATING PRODUCTS

This book has concentrated on the ledgers of the Pegasus accounting system, and it should not be forgotten that they are only part of a completely integrated business software suite of programs, that handle many associated data processing functions, including stock control, invoicing, order processing, payroll, job costing, sales history, fixed assets and retail accounting. Each of these are modules in their own right and can be linked together as an integrated solution to most processing requirements. Figure 8.2 shows an integration chart for Pegasus Single-User, while Figure 8.3 shows the same chart for Senior. The level of integration of Senior products is slightly more extensive, with additional modules over Single-User.

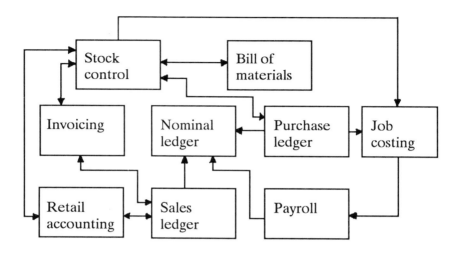

Figure 8.2   Single-User Integrated System

By extending your existing system by adding modules, the additional integration may prove beneficial. For example, adding a computerised payroll system means that salaries, pensions and other payroll-related information can be transferred to the nominal ledger.

TRAINING

Getting more out of your system has so far been about extending its data processing facilities, either by adding new modules, using another integrating software package or designing your own add-on application using a database product. However, there is another aspect to obtaining more from your system, and that is a matter of training. Some of the functions and features of the software system discussed in this book are those that tend to be overlooked, not just because of a shortage of time and resources,

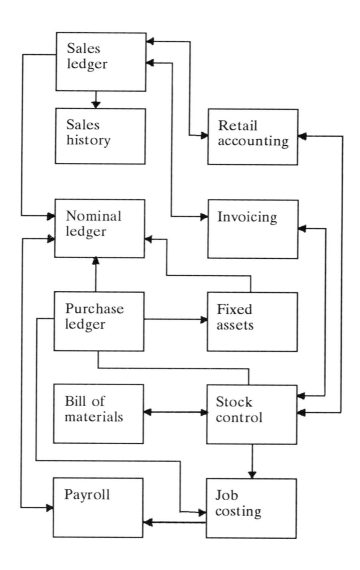

Figure 8.3   Senior Integrated System

but because of a lack of suitable and adequate training from one source or another. Training individuals who are responsible for the operation of the accounting ledgers is as much a part of the installation process as any other.

The training needs to comprehensively cover the functions of the system, and not just the basic processing of entering new accounts and their associated transactions. This means including the report generator, analysis facilities, integration, document design procedures, etc. Furthermore, there are still many users of accounting systems whose knowledge of the accounting principles themselves are either sparse or non-existent. Accounting systems help greatly in processing the accounts of an organisation, but they do not do the accounting for you as such.

You must at least understand the basic principles of book-keeping and, before designing the profit and loss and balance sheet layouts, understand the structure of accounts and the nature of the debits and credits recorded in them. Most of the documen-tation that accompanies Pegasus products gives little or no guid-ance on accounting principles, and assumes knowledge in this area for the most part. The actual level of knowledge needed by any individual operator will naturally depend upon their responsibil-ities. An invoice entry clerk will not require the same degree of book-keeping knowledge as the individual in charge of the nomi-nal ledger.

To get the best from your accounting ledgers requires an invest-ment in training for the individuals responsible, and this can be obtained either through your dealer or from independent author-ised Pegasus training centres. Information about these can be obtained from your dealer or directly from Pegasus Software Limited.

DEVELOPMENT OF SOFTWARE

One should always remember that the standard software packages are continually being enhanced and developed, with new features being added all the time. Improvements to the Pegasus systems come from the information supplied by the users themselves, who ask for input to the system to solve particular processing requirements.

Not all changes and developments produced get filtered through to the customers of Pegasus Software Limited, and information about new releases may not always find its way to the right individual. It is therefore as well to be aware that the development process takes place and perhaps a periodical enquiry to your dealer about new features may be a worthwhile exercise. The author knows of a company who was using Pegasus for some time without the report generator facility, which had been available for almost two years by then. When they found out what it could do, they saved themselves hours of additional accounting and paperwork. The obvious frustration was that had they known about the feature when it was released, they could have profited from it from the outset.

However, there are cases like this where the information about a new feature does not mean much to the reader until the function is demonstrated, and this is one reason why emphasis should be placed on tackling the dealers for information about new facilities. This may seem as though you are carrying out the dealers' sales activities for them, but you have to take the view of the advantages that may be gained for your own organisation as a result of a new software development.

As a final point regarding software development, should you seek to acquire a vertical market software application that integrates with Pegasus, or if your dealer produces an add-on application that integrates with the accounting system, make absolutely sure you understand what provisions are made in the case of enhancements to the Pegasus system and what impact this could have on your specially written application.

For example, some changes in the Pegasus systems result in changes to the layout and structure of the files. If your special application reads the data files of Pegasus and you upgrade your software to a new version of Pegasus, your original application may be unable to work any more. Be very careful to know exactly where you stand as far as support and ongoing maintenance are concerned with these add-ons, because Pegasus Software Limited themselves do not guarantee or support anything other than their own products.

Appendix A

Senior and Single-User Comparison

The following pages show some of the main differences between the features and functions of Pegasus Single-User and Senior sales, purchase and nominal ledgers. The information is as provided by Pegasus Software Limited, and may be subject to changes without prior notice from them. You are advised to check the latest details if you are considering changing from Single-User to Senior software.

General	Single-User	Senior
Colour monitor option	yes	yes
Report generator	yes	yes
Record capacity	32,000	65,000
Multi-currency	no	yes
Help facility	no	yes
Searching for a name	yes	yes
Scrolling on account code	yes	yes
Automatic backup facility	yes	yes
Log file	no	yes
Printer definitions	1	3
Password levels	1	4
Multiple VAT rates	no	yes
Parameter file help definition	yes	yes
Number of decimal places	2	0 to 4
Free file reset	no	yes
Version number check facility	yes	yes

User-defined tax description	yes	yes
Company parameter file	no	yes
Multi-company	no	yes
Direct link to Multiplan	yes	yes
Direct link to Lotus 1-2-3	yes	yes
Output in CSV file format	yes	yes
Screen and spooler options	yes	yes

Sales ledger	**Single-User**	**Senior**
Integration to nominal	yes	yes
Maximum no of customers	32,000	65,000
Maximum no of transactions	32,000	65,000
Accounts:		
Account code size	4	8
Account name length	30	30
Analysis code size:		
Sales account code	2	4
Product analysis code	4	8
Contact name and telephone	yes	yes
Credit limit maximum value	999,999	999,999
Open item/balance forward	yes	yes
Delete accounts with 0 balance	yes	yes
Transactions:		
Maximum value per posting	999,999.99	99,999,999.99
Maximum value per account	9,999,999.99	999,999,999.99
Maximum value per ledger	99,999,999.99	999,999,999.99
Calculated settlement disc	yes	yes
Max entries per receipt	50	no limit
Max entries per allocation	50	no limit
Max analysis lines per invoice	10	10
VAT cash accounting	yes	no
Match adjustments	no	yes
Advance postings	no	yes

Analysis:

No of definable reports	3	6
Levels of total in reports	2	3
VAT analysis	yes	yes

Reports:

Statements	fixed format	free format
Single shot statements	·no	yes
List invoices/credit notes	yes	yes
List receipts and adjustments	yes	yes
Aged debtors report	yes	yes
List of accounts	yes	yes
VAT outstanding report	yes	no
Label printing	yes (single)	yes (multiple)
Account history	yes	yes

Purchase ledger	**Single-User**	**Senior**
Integration to nominal	yes	yes
Maximum no of suppliers	32,000	65,000
Maximum no of transactions	32,000	65,000

Accounts:

Account code size	4	8
Account name length	30	30

Analysis code size:

Purchase account code	2	4
Product analysis code	4	8

Contact name and telephone	yes	yes
Credit limit maximum value	999,999	999,999
Open item/balance forward	yes	yes
Delete accounts with 0 balance	yes	yes

Transactions:

Maximum value per posting	999,999.99	99,999,999.99
Maximum value per account	9,999,999.99	999,999,999.99

Maximum value per ledger	99,999,999.99	999,999,999.99
Calculated settlement disc	yes	yes
Max entries per payment	50	no limit
Max entries per allocation	50	no limit
Max analysis lines per invoice	10	10
VAT cash accounting	yes	no
Match adjustments	no	yes
Advance postings	no	yes
Dispute facility	yes	yes
Detailed VAT validation	no	yes

Analysis:

No of definable reports	3	6
Levels of total in reports	2	3
VAT analysis	yes	yes

Reports:

Remittance advices	fixed format	free format
Single shot statements	no	yes
List invoices/credit notes	yes	yes
List payments and adjustments	yes	yes
Aged creditors report	yes	yes
List of accounts	yes	yes
Suggested payments list	yes	yes
Currency discrepancy list	no	yes
Label printing	yes (single)	yes (multiple)
Account history	yes	yes
Print cheques	yes	yes
Automatic payments	yes	yes

Nominal ledger	**Single-User**	**Senior**
Integration to sales/purchase	yes	yes
Maximum no of nominal a/cs	32,000	65,000
Maximum no of transactions	32,000	65,000

Accounts:

Account code size	4	8

Number of group headings:

1 character	36	36
2 characters	1,296	1,296
Cost centres	no	yes
Period budgets	no	yes
Budget factors	no	yes

Historical data:

Prior year actual	no	yes
Prior year budget	no	yes
This year actual	yes	yes
This period budget	total only	yes
Variance from budget	yes	yes

Transactions:

Max value per posting	999,999.99	99,999,999.99
Max value per account	9,999,999.99	999,999,999.99
Max value per ledger	99,999,999.99	999,999,999.99
Max entries per journal	49	50
Recurring journals	no	yes
Reversal of special journals	removal	reversal
Carry forward balance sheet	no	yes
Multiple bank accounts	no	yes
Bank reconciliation	yes	no

Reports:

Consolidation facility	no	yes
Consolidation from different currencies	no	yes
Audit trail on reserves and provisions	no	yes
No lines in P/L and balance sheet design	80 each	200 each
Number of report codes	84 each	148 each
List of transactions	yes	yes
List of accounts	yes	yes
List of cost centres	no	yes

List of budgets	no	yes
Cumulative expense analysis	no	yes
Historical expense analysis	no	yes
Trial balance	yes	yes
Profit and loss	yes	yes
Balance sheet	yes	yes

Appendix B

Transaction Pointer Example

This appendix gives an example of how transaction pointers work on a hypothetical file, and demonstrates how 'transaction gaps' can occur.

Names file:			Transaction file:			
	(pointers changed by each transaction)				Next pointer	
A/c no	First trans	Last trans	Trans no	A/c	Initial	Final
A001	1	1	1	A001		2
A001	1	2	2	A001		4
A002	3	3	3	A002		5
A001	1	4	4	A001		8
A002	3	5	5	A002		7
A003	6	6	6	A003		10
A002	3	7	7	A002		9
A001	1	8	8	A001		11
A002	3	9	9	A002		
A003	6	10	10	A003		
A001	1	11	11	A001		

Initially, for the first transaction on A001, there will be a blank pointer (ie no 'next' transaction pointer). The system will enter, on the names file, the first and last transaction numbers and they will both be 1.

If the second transaction is also for A001, the system will first of all look at the names file to find the last transaction number used for this item (ie 1). It will then enter the next transaction number (2) against the next transaction pointer of the previous transaction. Similarly, with the 4th transaction being A001 again, the system will look in the names file at A001, see that the last transaction number was 2, go to transaction number 2 in the transaction file and enter 4 as the next transaction pointer.

Thus, as the example shows, A001 in the transaction file will have a series of pointers, which point to all the transactions relating to A001. This will also apply to all other account numbers in use.

The effect of this is that, when the system is required to produce a report based on the account number reference, then the search for all transactions for each account number will be fast and efficient.

Of course, each time the system is accessed, it needs to know what the next transaction is. This is stored in the parameter file of each module. This record is written to the parameter file each time a process is terminated — ie if transaction number 12 has just been entered, then the number of the next transaction record in the parameter file will be incremented to 13 when the process is terminated.

TRANSACTION GAPS

The next transaction number is held in the computer's memory until the system is terminated to the main menu (not sub-menu), whereupon it is written to the parameter file. Thus, if another data disk is inserted at a sub-menu level and a transaction is made, then the next transaction number issued to that disk will be the one stored in memory. If, on this 'foreign' disk, the last transaction number was 5, then the next transaction number will be 13 (from the previous example), thus causing what is called a transaction gap. Subsequently, the next transaction pointer will be incremented to 14, and if the original disk is now reinserted, transaction number 13 will be missing, thus causing another transaction gap.

When called upon to produce a list of transactions, the system will stop at the transaction gap, and think it has reached the last transaction. The system will in fact be incapable of printing a list of transactions beyond that gap, until such time as the records are cleared by the period-end routine and the new period's transactions are entered.

Appendix C

Sample Chart of Nominal Accounts

Setting up the nominal chart of accounts requires some planning. For those organisations that have already got a tried and tested method of referencing accounts, it is possible that the existing system can be transferred to the account coding structure (and in the case of Senior, account and cost centre coding structure) without the need for adjustment. The same may be true if changing from one accounting system to another. For companies using a computerised nominal ledger for the first time, it can be useful to have a guide to work to, at least initially, and this appendix provides a sample chart of account structures suitable for a variety of types of business. This chart can be adapted, copied or extended to suit your individual requirements. The system is based on the Single-User account coding which is four characters. Senior uses eight characters in the account code with a further four available as a cost centre code. Adaptation of this list to Senior nominal ledger should be quite straightforward, if indeed there is any need to change the codes at all (there is no reason why all characters of a code should be used just because they exist).

For each section of the accounts, a heading account has been defined, based on the first two characters with trailing zeros. To use the facility in this way, the relevant parameter option needs to be set for using the first two characters for sub-totalling and header account purposes. In the case of Single-User this is nominal parameter option 8, and for Senior it is nominal parameter option 2.

Note: header accounts are specified first, with trailing zeros, and accounts are indented beneath.

A100   Long term assets

A101	Property cost
A102	Property depreciation
A103	Plant and machinery cost
A104	Plant and machinery depreciation
A105	Tools cost
A106	Tools depreciation
A107	Office equipment cost
A108	Office equipment depreciation
A109	Furniture, fixtures and fittings cost
A110	Furniture, fixtures and fittings depreciation
A111	Vehicles cost
A112	Vehicles depreciation

A200   Other long term and fixed assets

A201	Goodwill
A202	Patents and copyrights cost
A203	Patents and copyrights depreciation
A204	Investments quoted
A205	Investments unquoted
A206	Loans given
A207	Stock account
A208	Work in progress

A300   Current assets

A301	Debtors control account
A302	Sundry debtors
A303	Provision for doubtful debts
A304	Dividends receivable
A305	Outstanding share capital

A400 Taxation

A401 Input VAT
A402 Input VAT part exempt
A403 Recoverable income tax

A500 Deposits and cash

A501 Bills receivable
A502 Money on call
A503 Council loans
A504 Building society deposits
A505 Post-dated cheques
A506 Bank deposit account
A510 Current bank account
A511 Petty cash account

A600 Prepayments and adjustments

A601 Prepaid expenses
A602 Clearing account
A603 Asset adjustments
A604 Asset suspense account

BC00 Bank charges and interest

BC01 Bank interest paid
BC02 Bank charges
BC03 Currency exchange losses
BC04 Loan interest repaid
BC05 Hire purchase interest

C100 Cost of sales

C101 Material cost of sales
C102 Direct labour
C103 Indirect labour
C104 Carriage inward
C105 Duty

ED00   Expenses — depreciation

ED01	Property depreciation
ED02	Plant/machinery depreciation
ED03	Tools depreciation
ED04	Office equipment depreciation
ED05	Furniture, fixtures and fittings depreciation
ED06	Vehicle depreciation
ED07	Patents and copyrights depreciation

ES00   Expenses — sales

ES01	Fuel and oil
ES02	Vehicle servicing
ES03	Vehicle repairs/spares
ES04	Road fund licences
ES05	Vehicle insurance
ES06	Travelling expenses
ES07	Car hire
ES08	Hotel expenses
ES09	Entertainment — UK
ES10	Entertainment — overseas
ES11	Sales promotion campaigns
ES12	Advertising
ES13	Promotional gifts
ES14	Samples
ES15	Carriage outward
ES16	Packaging
ES17	Sales reps' commission

EX00   General expenses

EX01	Discount allowed
EX02	Bad debts
EX03	Provision for doubtful debts
EX04	Rent and rates
EX05	Rent
EX06	Water rates
EX07	General rates

EX08	Buildings insurance
EX09	Electricity
EX10	Gas
EX11	Oil
EX12	Repairs and renewals
EX13	Cleaning premises
EX14	Printing and stationery
EX15	Postage
EX16	Telephone
EX17	Telex
EX18	Stationery — office supplies
EX19	Journals, magazines, books
EX20	Equipment hire
EX21	Office machine maintenance
EX22	Donations
EX23	Subscriptions
EX24	Protective clothing
EX25	Stock adjustments
EX26	Machinery maintenance

L100   Liabilities

L101	Ordinary shares
L102	Preference shares
L103	Share premium account
L104	General reserves
L105	Undistributed profit
L106	Debentures
L107	Mortgages
L108	Loans received
L109	Hire purchase
L110	Creditors control account
L111	Sundry creditors
L112	Bills payable
L113	Accruals
L114	PAYE
L115	NI
L116	Wages/salaries
L117	Pensions

L200   Taxation liabilities

    L201   Output VAT − rate 1 (15%)
    L202   VAT payable

L300   Directors accounts

    L301   Directors loan account
    L302   Directors current account
    L303   Drawings account

L400   Dividends

    L401   Proposed dividend

LP00   Legal and professional expenses

    LP01   Legal fees
    LP02   Audit and accountancy fees
    LP03   Consultancy fees

P100   Purchases − materials

    P101   Purchases − general
    P102   Purchases − equipment
    P103   Purchases at zero % VAT
    P104   VAT exempt purchases

PF00   Profit brought forward

    PF01   Profit brought forward

S100   Sales/income accounts

    S101   Home sales
    S102   Export sales
    S103   VAT exempt sales
    S104   Sales at zero % VAT
    S105   Sundry trading income

S200   Non-trading income

S201   Royalties
S202   Interest
S203   Investment grants
S204   Sales of assets
S205   Currency exchange gains
S206   Discount received
S207   Commissions
S208   Recovered bad/doubtful debts
S209   Insurance claims
S210   Rent income

SS00   Suspense accounts

SS01   Debtors suspense account
SS02   Creditors suspense account

WS00   Wages and salaries

WS01   Salaries
WS02   Wages — regular
WS03   Wages — casual
WS04   Employer's NI
WS05   Employer's pension contribution
WS06   Directors' remunerations

Index